Change and the Future
International System

Change and the Future International System

EDITED BY

DAVID S. SULLIVAN

AND MARTIN J. SATTLER

COLUMBIA UNIVERSITY PRESS
NEW YORK AND LONDON

Editors' Foreword

Will the polar icecaps have melted in 30 years, due to pollution-induced climatic changes, flooding continents? Are the world's oxygen supplies, fossil energy, and mineral resources being too rapidly depleted, while radioactive waste materials proliferate? Will unequal distribution of resources and technological capabilities continue to cause conflict in an increasingly overpopulated world? Is the sovereignty of nation states eroding under the impact of multi-national corporations? Is global interdependence growing while nuclear power and the definition of security requirements remain under the jurisdiction and control of nation states? These are some questions about the future international system which analysts and statesmen are beginning to confront. Karl Deutsch has said that statesmen of the 19th century seemed to know what they were doing, but that during the 20th century runaway problems emerged. Some analysts argue that the major forces of social, ecological, and technological changes are now beyond the control of the world's political processes and leadership. If negotiations are achieving a relatively stable strategic balance despite technological advances, the most explosive division in the interdependent world seems no longer to be simply East versus West but resource-hungry rich countries versus poor. Maintenance of the ever-climbing level of living standards in the advanced countries, based on heavy energy and resource consumption, has raised the problem of somehow managing the biosphere on a global basis. The problem of political control of technology and its effects is the major theme of this issue of the JOURNAL. The contributors have tried to answer in varied ways some of the above questions which are transforming international politics.

In the first article, Bernard Brodie offers some insights into the difficulties involved in historical uncertainty and predictions about technology in the future international system. Rational prediction and scientific forecasting are probably the most difficult, yet among the most important, functions of the policy-maker and political scientist. Brodie points out the necessity for analysis of intention as well as capability in order to cope with the arms race realistically. He argues that there is an "asymptotic factor" limiting the political effects of technological change, and he applies this factor especially to nuclear weapons. These weapons help to deter limited war as well as nuclear war, and he discusses their role in regard to the NATO Alliance. In Brodie's view, the world's most pressing problem, which is itself a function of technology, is overpopulation. He nevertheless sees the primary potential causes of international conflict in the rich nations, not in the poor.

In the second article, Robert C. North and Nazli M. Choucri probe deeply into the relationships between politics and technology, an undertaking which Brodie calls for in his conclusion. Through their "demands equation," North-Choucri propose a useful definition of the "lateral pressure" concept which portrays the technologically advanced countries as huge vacuum cleaners sucking up the world's resources. Technology is seen as the "multiplier" of power, but enormous political, social, and environmental costs result from its development. Uneven access to resources, and differences in levels of population and technological development among states, are seen as the primary causes of international conflict. This analysis is broader than the deterministic analyses of American "economic imperialism" advanced by such revisionist historians as Gabriel Kolko, William A. Williams and Gar Alperovitz, because North-Choucri apply the concept of lateral pressure (technological imperialism) to all advanced countries regardless of ideology, political-economic system, or social structure. This lateral pressure concept also seems to contrast with the views of Herman Kahn, who has said that 95% of the traditional reasons for war among advanced nations have disappeared. The lesser developed countries of the Third World comprise the locus of the "points of intersection" of lateral pressure, the arena of Great Power competition. This view also contrasts somewhat with Brodie's, especially in regard to the Middle East. Some analysts note that two countries with rather weak ties to the Third World, Germany and Japan, had the highest growth rates in the 1950's, implying that the LDC's may have no essential short-term impact on an advanced nation's rate of growth. Others argue that the growing population in the countryside of the Third World cannot be readily mobilized, either economically or politically, and is, therefore, not of much international importance.

North-Choucri argue that because international conflict is a function of the "demands equation," political scientists should study the budgets of governments and analyze resource allocation. Military allocations are seen as especially dysfunctional because they stimulate resource acquisition and depletion, thereby generating the international conflict they are intended to counteract. North-Choucri conclude pessimistically that because the basic causes of war lie deeply rooted in lateral pressures resulting from uneven resource distribution, mediation, conciliation, international law and organizations are all insufficient for the preservation of peace. Neither national nor international political processes can now control the *underlying* causes of lateral pressure, yet there seems to be a great requirement for an international security regulator to control lateral pressure itself. This in turn implies an eventual necessity for some kind of international control of technology, of access to resources, and of population growth.

In the third article, Herbert S. Dinerstein takes a unique historical approach to ideology in alliance systems, comparing the Communist Party of the Soviet Union in the international communist movement to the Catholic Church of the Counter Reformation. The comparative roles of ideology are analyzed in regard to legitimization, perceptions of reality and interests, "military-industrial complexes," the Viet Nam War, the Thirty Years' War, Czechoslovakia, Germany, China, and the Third World. He concludes that Western restraint (containment having predominated over "rollback") made the socialist camp safe for heresy and diversity, thus increasing possibilities for intra-communist schisms. These heresies and hostilities within the international communist movement are more virulent than communist opposition to "capitalist" nations, but this polycentric situation only came to be appreciated in the West after the Viet Nam War had begun. In Dinerstein's view, nuclear weapons have resulted in a stabilized "adversary" relationship between the U.S. and the U.S.S.R. He concludes by suggesting a concentric circle model of the future international system.

In the fourth article, Eugene B. Skolnikoff posits a model for the functions of international organizations in dealing with the problems of technology in the future. He suggests that national sovereignty is breaking down, due to the growth of an international technology and culture. While agreeing with Brodie that overpopulation is the world's greatest problem, he analyzes the almost equally pressing international problems in food production, pollution, resource depletion, utilization of the seas and outer space, and climatic change. Skolnikoff concludes that solutions or palliatives for these vast and growing problems can only be found in developing the functions of international organizations, and through technology itself.

In the fifth article, William D. Coplin's analysis and conclusions largely parallel Skolnikoff's. Coplin compares the development of interwar and postwar international organizations, presenting a developmental model of their roles in the international bargaining process for *collectively* solving the problems of technology. Coplin agrees with Brodie and Dinerstein that the existence of nuclear weapons greatly decreases the likelihood of general war. He optimistically minimizes the effects of territorial, symbolic, and ideological issues upon the likelihood of future international conflict and does not consider the concept of lateral pressures by technologically advanced states. In contrast to Skolnikoff, Coplin argues that it is necessary to insulate technological problems from domestic politics in order to deal with them collectively on the international level. Increasing global interdependence should thus lead to a globalization of decision-making.

Finally, Tilden J. LeMelle and George W. Shepherd, Jr. analyze the much neglected factor of racial stratification in international politics, particularly the ramifications of centripetal and centrifugal white-dominance political systems. By focusing upon racism as an underlying cause of both Western and Soviet imperialism, their analysis also contrasts with the revisionist school. LeMelle-Shepherd largely support the conclusions of North-Choucri, Skolnikoff, and Coplin concerning the necessity for international regulation of access to resources in order to lessen conflict both within the Third World itself and between advanced and poor states. They all have neglected, however, consideration of present or potential capabilities of LDC's to make use of technology and resources. Further, LeMelle-Shepherd point out the significant potentialities for revolutionary war in the Third World.

Revolutionary war is largely ignored by Brodie; North-Choucri's concept of lateral pressure also apparently fails to account for it. Revolutionary war, with racial origins, could take place in the Third World arena of Great Power competition with states or ethnic groups acting as proxies for the Powers, as Dinerstein implies. Or revolutionary war could be an intrastate phenomenon within racially stratified, exploited Third World states themselves, as LeMelle-Shepherd suggest. Their analysis of the effects of domestic racism upon foreign policy is noteworthy. Like North-Choucri, they use Sweden as an ideal model for future social systems.

Taken together, these articles offer a sound approach to understanding some of the momentous problems which will shape the future international system; but as Skolnikoff observes, this is only a beginning.

Contents

Change and the Future
International System

BERNARD BRODIE

The Impact of Technological Change on the International System: Reflections on Prediction

Who knows what the international system will look like 50 years hence, and how it will be affected by a technology which itself requires a certain boldness to predict? The existing international system, insofar as it has been affected by the technology of our time, was not predictable with any appreciable confidence as recently as thirty years ago; it would have seemed a fanciful and even outlandish construction to the observer of 60 years ago, who was yet to experience World War I.

Yet, because prediction is inherent in any policy recommendation, decision, or criticism, a major goal of political science is prediction and continuing improvement of the predictive processes. The recommendation or the criticism reflects the belief, which may or may not be explicit, that certain consequences, good or bad, are likely to follow from the policy urged or denounced. Or the criticism may simply restate uncertainty about the consequences—itself a form of prediction—and demand that the uncertainty be accounted for and its adverse effects minimized in the policy decision itself.[1] The sophisticated handling of uncertainty has been an im-

[1] See the work of the French political economist, Bertrand de Jouvenal, *Art of Conjecture* (New York: Basic Books, 1967); also the yearbook which he edits, *Futuribles: Studies in*

Bernard Brodie, formerly of the graduate faculty of Yale University and subsequently a Senior Staff Member of The RAND Corporation, has returned to the academic world as Professor in the Department of Political Science, University of California at Los Angeles. He is the author of several well-known and widely used books, including STRATEGY IN THE MISSILE AGE. He has just completed a manuscript for a new book, to be entitled STRATEGY AND POLITICS.

1

portant part of that modern development known as systems analysis. Thus far mostly applied to the selection of weapons systems, systems analysis is quite consciously an effort at scientific prediction; that is, one predicts that one system will suit certain specified purposes better than one or more proposed alternatives.[2]

However, if we admit that policy-making involves prediction, hopefully responsible and sophisticated prediction, and that policy-making is what we are mainly concerned about as citizens and as political scientists, we are also delimiting the kinds of prediction in which we are interested. Random speculation about the future may be interesting as a diversion, but it is usually idle if it has no policy implications, which is to say if it does not stem from the decision-making process. It offers little inducement for the kind of cautious and painstaking treatment of uncertainty and the careful information-gathering involved in good decision-making. An occasional shot in the dark may prove correct. But one has to ask: was it a *serious* prediction, legitimately claiming enough chance of fulfillment to warrant its affecting a relevant policy decision?

We derive from the policy-making function of prediction various means of controlling our exposure to speculative risk. Perhaps the most important control concerns the factor of time. We give kudos to statesmen for being "far-sighted," and it is right that we should. However, it makes some difference whether being far-sighted concerns a situation 100 years away or one only 5 or 10 years away. Actually, the statesman's business rarely requires him to look ahead as much as 30 years, and by far the greater part of his decisions are projected for time periods that are very much shorter. The payoff for the correct decision is generally expected to begin relatively soon, even when the policy adopted has longer-term implications.

We have heard a good deal to the contrary, especially from the systems analysts advising on choices of weapons systems. In that area, we are al-

---

Conjecture, Vol. 1, (Geneva: Droz, 1963). Other books on approaches and methods in prediction are G. R. Bright, ed., *Technological Forecasting for Industry and Government* (New York: Prentice-Hall, 1968); William F. Butler and Robert A. Kavesh, eds., *How Business Economists Forecast* (New York: Prentice-Hall, 1966); Olaf Helmer, *Social Technology* (New York: Basic Books, 1965); Erich Jantsch, *Technological Forecasting in Perspective* (Paris: OECD, 1967); Robert W. Prehoda, *Designing the Future: The Role of Technological Forecasting* (Philadelphia: Chilton Book Corp., 1967); and Michael Young, *Forecasting and the Social Sciences* (London: Heineman, 1968). See also the many papers on the subject by Dr. Yehezkel Dror issued by the The RAND Corp., especially "The Prediction of Political Feasibility," p-4044 (Santa Monica: April, 1969), and his book, *Public Policy-Making Reexamined* (New York: Chandler, 1968).

[2] The literature on systems analysis is by now fairly extensive, but among basic books on the subject, I recommend E. S. Quade, ed., *Analysis for Military Decisions*, The RAND Corp., R-387-PR, 1964, and C. J. Hitch and R. N. McKean, *The Economics of Defense in the Nuclear Age* (Cambridge, Mass.: Harvard University Press, 1960).

ways being reminded of the inexorable demands of lead times, of the fact that whatever system we opt for now will not be available for some 6 to 8 years, after which it is expected to have a life span which will justify its cost. The emphasis is on thinking ahead and on making timely decisions. However, the development process is begun with the knowledge that it is subject to change, that is, to acceleration, retardation, augmentation, or cancellation. Often the total political context will indicate to the politically sensitive a much smaller risk in postponing a decision than the weapons-oriented technologists are conditioned to believe.[3] Even after a weapons system is deployed it can be readily phased out again if there is the freedom to decide that it was an error or that it has been made obsolete by other developments.

That freedom, though usually imperfect, is nevertheless greater than the freedom to change our minds about political commitments, where we never hear anything about lead times. If we ask how we are now affected by dubious decisions made 15 or more years ago in the national security field, those which concerned weapons systems seem today to matter relatively little. It has proved far simpler and also much less costly to phase out an obsolete or ill-advised weapons system than to phase out a comparably depreciated political commitment—even such a relatively modest one as that which has subsidized Franco's Spain for the sake of our bomber bases. One reason for this is that it is usually considered virtuous not to recognize or acknowledge the possibility of error or of decay of justification in an alliance-type commitment.

In retrospect some decisions loom as landmarks in a long historical process, but that does not necessarily mean that the men who made them were weighing the very long view against the short. President Lincoln's decision to oppose secession even by force of arms was bound to have major consequences into the distant future, but it also had shorter-term consequences as well, and our image of Lincoln would not suffer from knowing

---

[3] The customary refrain of these analysts, enthusiastically supported by their military clients, is: We are interested in the opponent's capabilities, not his intentions. Presumably intentions cannot be known but only guessed at, and are anyway subject to sudden change (implicitly, always for the worse), while capabilities are in the main observable and measurable—and in being so they can signal trends. Moreover, whatever the opponent's intentions, his capabilities must not be ignored. I have commented on this argument at some length in my *Escalation and the Nuclear Option* (Princeton, N.J.: Princeton University Press, 1966), Ch. 7, "On Enemy Capabilities Versus Intentions." Let me repeat here, however, that while this view is not without merit—certainly we cannot disregard the enemy's capabilities—it grossly and excessively depreciates both our ability to gauge the opponent's intentions and the importance of doing so. It thus clearly favors a bias toward increasing armaments, the more so because those who advance it most vigorously are habitually insensitive to the way one's own armaments programs may look to the opponent. It is, in short, the doctrine which powers armaments races.

that he was thinking mostly about the latter. He was choosing a great war *now,* and it would hardly have behooved him to justify his action by boldly (and presumptuously) postulating the consequences some 100 years hence.

War is unique in being that situation where statesmen often appear to be appealing to very long-term interests, likely enough nebulous or fictitious, in order to justify inordinately heavy short-term costs. Though the psychology of motivation in such instances is complicated, there is plenty of evidence to suggest that the leader who makes a bold decision for war is very much concerned with how he looks *now* to himself and to others. True, this decision may be in simple fulfillment of a commitment which appeared to have a long-term outlook, but insofar as such commitments have a clear and rational purpose, their justification is usually put in terms of "from *here* on out." In matters not concerning war, statesmen will often choose one course of action over another because they believe it to be "in the right direction," that is, having some promise of eventual rather than short-term payoff—but as a rule only if the short-term costs are sufficiently modest.

Thus, if we try to foresee the effects of technological changes on the future international system, it is both useless and unnecessary to attempt to look far into the future, because it is rare that a policy decision requires it. If one can think of a decision that does appear to require long-range prediction, a closer look will often indicate that the decision were better postponed. Naturally, this thought offers no excuse for the continuing neglect of problems for which it requires no great predictive sagacity to realize that the undesirable effects are inexorable and cumulative—as is true of a variety of urban and ecological problems and of the population explosion.

Some of the best and most useful predictions, especially of the effects of technology, have not been so much predictions as clear-eyed perceptions of what was currently going on and where it was leading us. With good eyesight one has less need of a crystal ball. Fortunately, good perception is subject to improvement by appropriate learning and experience, while the gift of prophecy is proverbially associated with divine grace.

A related point is not sufficiently considered in most efforts at prediction—which is remarkable because it greatly simplifies our task. In various important categories of technology, we may expect that future improvements even of the most ingenious kind will not have social and political consequences remotely comparable to those achieved in the past. There is, in other words, a kind of asymptote of influence in any category of technology beyond which change becomes more or less free-wheeling, interesting to engineers and often to economists but not to political scientists.

This situation is no doubt already upon us with respect to the technologies of verbal communications and transportation. For the movement of people, the change from sail to steam and then to air, culminating in jet-propelled aircraft, is one thing. The change from the latter to anything else remotely conceivable is bound to be immeasurably less important politically. The first argument against the SST, for example, is not ecological but simply that it buys the passengers nothing that is at all worth the additional cost, assuming it is they, and not the taxpayers, who will pay those costs. This very marginal diminution of time in transporting even the most important passengers could hardly affect the relations between nations. We can now even transport two men at a time to the surface of the moon, naturally at speeds far exceeding that of the SST, but the political consequences of this fabulous technological accomplishment seem to be about nil.

These considerations apply even more to the transport of commodities. Except for some few perishable or high-cost luxury goods, it is transportation cost, rather than speed, which matters. It came as a surprise to many that the closing of the Suez Canal as a result of the Six Day War in 1967 seemed to have so little effect on ocean trade. The use of increasingly larger ships is the trend in ocean transport, especially for carrying oil, where ships of 250,000 deadweight tons are already in use with additional ones being built in Japan, and where even larger ones are projected. With such ships, which are far too large to transit the canals, oil moves more cheaply from the Middle East to its major markets in Northern Europe, even though the journey around the Cape is much longer. But even transportation costs, both for commodities and for human beings, have fallen to such levels that it is difficult to see how any striking and *politically important* changes can result from achieving further economies. The impediments to international trade that matter today are rarely found in the costs of transportation, especially sea-borne transportation, but rather in deliberate restraints upon trade like tariffs and quotas.

The same is true of the communication of information, only more so. The conduct of diplomacy was indeed revolutionized by the development of world-wide telegraphic and telephonic communications, but what can result from further advances—like the perfecting of video telephones? In that connection, we have been hearing a good deal recently about the effects of television upon such things as the proclivity of the American people for violence, upon their attitudes toward the war in Vietnam, and so on. What we have not seen or heard is the slightest bit of evidence to support these often dogmatic assertions.

The asymptotic factor applies even to the effective changes in the nature of war. Herman Kahn has frequently remarked that since World War II there has been a complete revolution in weaponry every 4 or 5 years. If so, it has been apparent only to specialists. After the coming of nuclear weapons, which changed everything, no new weapons technology could quite matter as much politically—unless it cancelled out nuclear weapons, a highly unlikely development. True, nuclear weapons became thermonuclear, missiles of increasing accuracy replaced aircraft as the primary delivery vehicles, the numbers and technological sophistication of both weapons and delivery systems increased considerably, and now we have the ABM. All these changes have been significant and certainly costly. Still, the big political event was Hiroshima, and most of what has happened since simply confirms and underlines that fact.

No doubt the most pervasive effects of technology upon the international system have come and will continue to come from those fundamental changes which have basically altered the economies of the various nations. The 20th century differs most startlingly from the 19th, as the 19th did from the 18th, with respect to the technologies affecting the production of goods and services, and it is possible in retrospect to see how these aggregate changes stimulated changes in the political and social environment. But we can also see that the effects are often most indirect and always strongly influenced by cultural factors.

How can we predict the social, economic, and political effects of technological change in the future when we find it not at all easy to distinguish its effects in the past? The aristocratic caste that ruled the nations of Central and Eastern Europe well into this century seem in retrospect to have been clearly anachronistic by the time they produced the Great War which destroyed them, but by what criteria? One perhaps feels intuitively that it was modern technology that made them so, and yet the case is not easily made. As a class they were destroyed by World War I, and it was 20th century technology that made that war as fierce and all-consuming as it was. Would this caste have survived into our own time if they had only managed to avoid that desperate war? The answer to this historical question is not so important as the recognition of its complexity.

When we talk about the effects of technology upon some body of cultural or political phenomena, we usually prefer to fix our attention upon what we presume to be simpler and more obvious cause-and-effect relationships than those just described. There is no harm in that except that certain conclusions tend to become hackneyed long before it is established that they are correct. Certainly any denial of the complexity of the cause-and-effect relationship is not going to help us with our predictions.

The following pages briefly survey two of the more commonly expressed propositions about the future effects of technology on the international system. We shall reconsider their validity and meaning.

An old and familiar proposition holds that technological change influences international politics most momentously and certainly most conspicuously by its effects upon the conduct of war. This proposition seems unquestionably true when one considers how central to all international politics is the omnipresent spectre of war. And nothing is clearer than that the basic nature of war has indeed been changed by changing technology (though I have asserted above that further changes in nuclear technology cannot have much political meaning). What is remarkable is that while acceptance of this generalization is virtually universal, the idea seems really to have penetrated our analysis very little.

No one failed to notice that the coming of nuclear weapons, especially after they assumed thermonuclear form, "revolutionized warfare." But what has this meant in practice? How has it affected the relations of states with each other, especially of those we call the superpowers? Above all, how has it affected the probability of war between the superpowers, including China? Few questions are more vital than these in attempting to foresee the "future international system."

There has been plenty of speculation on these issues, but it has generally been shallow and glib with little attempt at serious exploration of the possible or likely consequences of this cosmic weaponry on the future state system. It is remarkable, for example, how readily the assumption is made that nuclear weapons have intensified the profound awfulness of war, "if they are used," without having much effect upon the inclination to resort to war! Nuclear weapons, it is alleged, deter only the opponent's resort to nuclear weapons, not his propensity to risk war—a notion that I consider to be profoundly *and obviously* wrong. During most of the years of his tenure, former Secretary of Defense Robert S. McNamara put heavy pressure on our NATO allies to accept a conception of a "likely" Soviet attack in Europe which, to guard against appropriately, would have required a massive and therefore costly build-up of conventional armaments. The idea that only nuclear armaments are exceedingly costly is one of the lesser absurdities of our time. For reasons I have detailed elsewhere, the contingencies against which our allies were being urged to provide very large sums of money and to tighten up or reintroduce conscription seemed to me wildly improbable. It was easily predictable that our allies simply would not go along with this peculiar American notion.[4] Without bothering to refute it—except by demanding, and receiving, periodic assurances that our nuclear weapons remained their ultimate safeguard—they did disregard it. Their doing so was indeed fortunate for us in several respects, especially in exerting a kind of feedback which helped to cool our ardor about increasing our own conventional forces, though not before the forces we had created helped get us involved in Vietnam.

Insofar as there was a public debate on the relevant issues, the ranks of the debaters were startlingly devoid of political scientists, even though the relevant speculations concerned not military but essentially political evaluations. Most of the men around Mr. McNamara who were promoting the cause of conventional build-up were systems analysts (mostly economists), and they carried with them various key members of sub-cabinet rank and of the higher bureaucracy, most of whom happened to be lawyers by training.

The same example can also serve for another important point applying to all policy-oriented predictions. We often hear that a certain contingency is "conceivable," and if what is "conceivable" would also be catastrophic, the presumption is that it warrants serious attention. At places like The RAND Corporation, the U.S. Government subsidizes a substantial corps of very bright young men whose function is largely to "conceive" of far-out possibilities, which they do very well. There can certainly be nothing objectionable about paying people to be imaginative, but we must know how to deal with the products of their imagination.

It is all very well to say that some ill which is "conceivable" ought to be countered, but if doing so requires a good deal of scarce resources, one wants to have some idea of how probable the "conceivable" ill really is. It is a commonplace idea in the insurance business that an extremely remote contingency deserves a small premium or none at all. True, if we are talking about thermonuclear strategic attack, which would be unutterably devastating if it occurred, it may make sense to spend large sums of money for additional deterrence, thereby reducing an attack probability as nearly as possible to the vanishing point. This surely is one of the major reasons why we are talking about providing an ABM defense. But we simply cannot afford to apply this kind of thinking to everything that is merely "conceivable."

The spectacle of a large Soviet field army crashing across the line into

---

[4] My own unequivocal predictions that our NATO allies would not accept and act upon the American doctrine was contained in my article: "What Price Conventional War Capabilities in Europe?," *The Reporter,* (May 23, 1963). See also my "How Not to Lead an Alliance," *The Reporter* (March 9, 1967), and my *Escalation and the Nuclear Option, op.cit.*

Western Europe in the hope *and expectation* that nuclear weapons would not be used against it—thereby putting itself and the U.S.S.R. totally at risk while leaving the choice of weapons to us—seems to me hardly worth a second thought, let alone the complete reorganization and very considerable expansion of our own and our allies' military forces. Why we should be eager to do everything in our power (almost certainly with little if any success) to encourage among the Russians an expectation that nuclear weapons would not be used in such circumstances, is still another question. We are, after all, trying to deter war, not merely the use of nuclear weapons. It is a curious thing that the people who were most in favor of the conventional build-up happened to be professionally dedicated to the idea that quantification *à outrance* is essential in all sorts of probability analysis, but on this issue they simply got religion and forgot probability analysis altogether.

In the security field, we are thinking in terms not of certainty, which if demanded can only be paralyzing, but of high probabilities warranting high-confidence predictions. There is a difference between being cautious in prediction and being conservative. While caution in prediction is always commendable, conservatism is usually a weakness. Caution applies to how many specifics of change we can foresee, not to the expectation of change or the readiness to be responsive to it, in which respects conservatism is generally negative.

Most judgments thus far about the political effects of nuclear weapons have been extremely conservative. We often hear that nuclear weapons have been "neutralized" or "decoupled" from the processes of international politics. On the contrary there seems to be abundant evidence that the superpowers never contemplate a power move vis-à-vis each other without being fully conscious of the fact that they live and will continue indefinitely to live in a nuclear-armed world. Instead of talking about nuclear weapons being "decoupled," we might begin at last to probe into what they really mean for the state system of the future.

The probability is extremely high that the superpowers will continue to operate with full understanding, which already exists and which hardly seems to need further development, that they cannot under any circumstances allow themselves to become involved in a major war with each other. There has been some posturing as though this understanding did not exist, but since the Cuban Missile Crisis of 1962 the disposition to this kind of posturing has sharply waned. There were already many other factors which tended to make resort to major war a much less "natural" means of resolving a critical impasse than it was before 1914, especially the experience of two world wars and the marked erosion, certainly in the

9

more developed nations, of views which still equated war with glory. However, nuclear weapons have made this assumption virtually final. To say that it is "not inevitable" that direct combat between the major nuclear powers would escalate into nuclear war is one thing. It has some, perhaps important, meaning. But it is very different from saying—and one certainly cannot now say—that we can have major fighting between the superpowers with high confidence that it will stay non-nuclear. The nations possessing powerful nuclear capabilities are not able to guarantee that they will never use them in war—and they are properly reluctant to offer such promises. Only through avoidance of major war can non-use be guaranteed. One might further observe that it does not appear possible, at least not within the next 30 years, that some new technological device will serve to neutralize nuclear weapons. It is surely wrong to expect such a result of the ABM, either of the present generation of related weaponry or of subsequent ones. We are confirmed in this prediction by our perennial experience with offensive versus defensive armament: technology marches forward on both these fronts, never only on one.

Just how the nations will adjust to this effective prohibition against major war—paradoxically the more effective for not being obviously 100 per cent certain—is less clear than that they will do so. There have been hints, both in the way the few real confrontations have been conducted and in the way in which they have been avoided. The rituals of what we have called limited war as practiced by us both in Korea and in Vietnam are only a part of the significant pattern that is emerging. Insofar as we find that these self-imposed limitations critically reduce our military effectiveness, the lesson will have to be not fewer limitations but fewer interventions. Thus, we have one more reason for concluding, despite frequent assertions to the contrary, that the nuclear arsenals must tend to deter not only nuclear wars but lesser wars as well.

The U.S. has indeed managed since World War II to engage in two other wars, not of the major category but considerable enough. It is worth noting, however, that the other superpower has not permitted itself to do the same. Our own experience in both cases, unsatisfactory in Korea and wholly agonizing in Vietnam, is clearly cooling the kind of ardor and the addiction to cold war shibboleths that led to these two interventions. The dire predictions of what might have happened to our vital interests had we not intervened in each case, moot at best, become markedly unconvincing—especially, of course, in Vietnam—when weighed against the total costs incurred by our intervening and the unsatisfactory nature of the results.

The second issue that is of comparable significance to the nuclear problem concerns one of the most clearly predictable of social and political phenomena, the population explosion. The direction is toward disaster. The problem has been created by technology, especially the technology of modern epidemiology. It has proved socially and politically far more acceptable to slow the death rate technologically than to limit births. We will soon have the problem of limiting massive starvation. But the trend is showing itself first as a fairly rapid rise in the *proportion* of the world's population, already almost two-thirds, which is desperately poor. It is hard to see how a decline in living conditions can be avoided among a large part of those very people who seem now not to have much room for further decline.

Solutions for population problems are impeded by some critical factors. First, we are desperately short of time. In some countries which are already feeling population pressure keenly, the proportion of young people is so high that it is presently impossible to see how the birth rate can be reduced fast enough to avoid a doubling of numbers within the next 25 years. That is true of much of South America, and of other areas as well. The Aswan Dam in Egypt was supposed to provide enough productive acreage to feed 8 million additional mouths, but population has increased by much more than this since work on the dam began. Now the predictions are that the Aswan Dam will itself create soil problems which will considerably reduce the net benefits formerly expected.

Scientists are now telling us not to expect any appreciable increase in the harvest of calories and proteins from the sea.[5] Unless we control oil and other pollution, we shall do well to maintain current levels of marine food production. So far as intensifying the production of food on land is concerned, the most important gains in the past 2 or 3 decades have been achieved in the realm of plant genetics. New breeds of grains have greatly increased yields where it has proved feasible and appropriate to use those breeds and where the supply of fertilizer could be increased. But further substantial gains will require first the application of considerable capital, mostly for the expansion and irrigation of arable land where such expansion is possible; this excludes much of the Orient.[6] Where is the capital to come from? The chapter in American history which included the

---

[5] See Paul R. Ehrlich and Anne H. Ehrlich, "The Food-From-The-Sea Myth," *The Saturday Review* (April 4, 1970). This article was taken from their *Population, Resources, Environment: Issues in Human Ecology* (San Francisco: Freeman and Co., 1970).

[6] See the paper by Professor Roger Revelle in *Overcoming World Hunger,* Proceedings of the Eleventh Air Force Academy Assembly, April 9-12, 1969.

Marshall Plan and subsequently large annual gifts of resources to countries all over the world appears to be drawing to a close, and it is difficult to be sanguine about aid revival, especially for cases which continue to look hopeless because of failures to control population growth. The future needs of the underdeveloped world far surpass anything that the wealth-sharing programs of the advanced nations can supply. Besides, it was Europe to which we gave Marshall Plan grants, and comparable efficiency and vigor in the use of foreign aid cannot be expected of the poorer countries of the world.

If capital accumulation is to come largely from areas that need it for their own salvation, we must first help them over a huge initial barrier. In some areas of the world, including large and populous India, the levels of food intake are already so low for most of the population that it is essential to increase them just so the population may have enough energy to raise itself by its bootstraps.[7] Whatever results are achieved in food production—and food is not the only resource limitation we have to be concerned about—they will have to be more than matched, and very soon, by achievements in humane birth limitation.[8] As John Kenneth Galbraith puts it, these "poor peasant" societies are all subject "to the same cruel parameters of over-population, insufficient land, insufficient capital, insufficient education, and a technology that is limited by all of these."

How the population crisis will affect the international system is another question. From the humanitarian point of view there can be no doubt that population control is the most serious problem that presently confronts us. It is a problem that has already been with us for some time, and

[7] In the above-cited paper Professor Revelle describes (p. 26) a dramatic demonstration of this fact in the building of the Mangla Dam in West Pakistan. The American contractors were unable to get more than about four hours of useful work per day out of the 10,000 native laborers hired. They tried the experiment of providing them with a supplementary lunch, after which they had no difficulty in getting a full 8 hours of productive work.

[8] Economists tend to discuss the issue mostly in terms of rate of economic growth, which, when measured against population growth, gives the net growth in average per capita income. However, apart from such questions as maldistribution of benefits from rate of income growth, there are special issues concerning food supply. Where people generally have extremely low per capita income, they are extremely vulnerable to increases in the price of food, i.e., a 2 per cent annual increase in per capita income can be swiftly nullified by a somewhat more than proportionate increase in the price of cereals, even if other consumers' goods show stable or diminishing prices. The rate of increase of food production experienced in the Far East over the last 2 decades simply cannot be expected to continue, but the rate of increase in the population remains inexorably steady—and high. For some excellent articles on economic growth in the underdeveloped areas, see *Journal of International Affairs*, Vol. XXIV, No. 2 (Summer, 1970), especially the articles by Richard Jolly, "The Aid Relationship: Reflections on the Pearson Report," and Stanislaw H. Wellisz, "The Implications of a Six Percent Growth Rate for Asia."

only the most determinedly optimistic do not consider its worsening to be inevitable. Thermonuclear war is by contrast only a possibility, and even if it happened the number of people directly affected would be far less than those fated to live lives of misery and want as a result of population pressure. On the other hand, in terms of its influence on international politics, it is not the same kind of potent issue that is posed by nuclear weapons.

The reasons for this statement are several. Nuclear weapons concern the superpowers directly, while population pressure is primarily a problem of those poorer nations which, because of their very poverty, have already been thrust far down the scale of influence. We have abundant evidence to indicate that people born to penury who are suffering malnutrition and attendant forms of want and misery usually do their suffering in a manner that permits their being ignored—especially since those who are even relatively well off want to ignore them, for reasons which must surely be regarded as understandable. The really poor are rarely politically effective, even in the domestic politics of their respective nations, let alone in international politics. The form of government seems less immediately relevant than the differences between competent and incompetent administration, though the differences between far left and far right probably look much more interesting to the peasant in the lower four-fifths of any poor society than they do to the well-fed citizens of our leading democracies, who can afford to reject both. We hear much more about Egypt's truculent hostility toward Israel than about the fact that most of its people have for a long time been living lives of desperate privation. Does the latter fact have anything to do with the truculence? It is doubtful that it does, except that the warfare with Israel probably helps those in power to escape emotionally from a domestic problem which they must find just too intractable.

Does severe population pressure and its attendant evils dispose a people or a nation toward aggression and war? Many demographers seem to assume that it does, that the future of the world is imperiled not only by the magnitude of the expected privation, but also by the aggression to which starving people will be impelled by their envy and despair. However, our experience with mankind and its wars, especially in modern times, does not seem to bear out so gloomy a prediction. What is practically unheard of in modern times is a poor country attacking a neighbor, presumably though not necessarily a wealthier country, in order to seize land for the better sustenance of its own people. We have had nations waging aggression in order to seize territories, but not for that reason.

The more typical pattern is that of World War II, where each of the Axis Powers was avowedly seeking expansion of its territories. These were nations at or near the top of the heap economically, especially Germany, and richly endowed with capital and other resources, which also made it more difficult to defeat them. Considering the make-up of the persons who were responsible for the aggressive policies of each of these nations, it is clear that what they were after was not a bigger supply of food for each future citizen, but the greater glory and prestige of the Fatherland. That has been the basis for the perennial drive for territorial aggrandizement over at least the last three centuries. The instances in which land is seized in order that one's own people should have more to farm are very exceptional, the outstanding modern example being the underpopulated and vigorous U.S. It moved westward the course of empire by taking land away from the poor Mexicans and the poorer Indians.

Really poor countries are usually too much weighed down with their internal problems and with the lethargy in the population which poverty induces, to be aggressive. Rich countries rather than poor ones generally make war, and certainly the increasing sophistication of modern weaponry will not enhance the military effectiveness of poor nations as against the advanced ones, except where the former become the pawns of the superpowers. If the poor nation is very large and also tightly and dictatorially organized, like China, rigorous allocation of resources into military purposes can make up for a very low per capita income and provide a respectable military capability. Still, Chinese power bears no comparison to that of the two superpowers, and the Chinese leaders have thus far conducted themselves as though they recognized very well that the solution of their domestic problems is not going to be achieved through foreign conquests. Besides, what large territories lie on their frontiers to be taken? The two large land masses on their borders belong to the powerful U.S.S.R. and to desperately poor, terribly over-populated India.

There can be a great deal of trouble in the world without its necessarily taking the form of war, or even being conducive to war. Also, the long, large history of mankind's wars shows unmistakably that among the predisposing factors to military aggression are full bellies, not empty ones.

How then may we summarize our findings? First, though it is almost impossible to make *serious* long-term predictions about technological developments, the needs of the policy-making function are usually satisfied with much shorter-term predictions. Second, it is one thing to predict technological developments, and quite another to forecast the *impact* of these developments on international political procedures or systems.

There are too many other factors operating to effect political changes, and besides, the influence of technological change is subject to what we have called the asymptotic factor. The latter is the simple but neglected idea that there is infinitely more difference between the carrier pigeon and radio telephony than between the latter and any conceivable alternative. With the coming of nuclear weapons, this asymptotic factor applies even to the development of techniques of war. Third, the huge problem of population pressure that is already with us is one of the few instances in which we can say that trends are "inevitable," and worsening. This problem has been created by technology and can be ameliorated by further technological developments, but not solved by them. Improved means of contraception are much more surely predictable than the development of mores which make threatened populations want to limit births. Finally, the greatest need in predicting the future is to be honest about uncertainty. Where uncertainties are compounded (as they always are when we go farther into the future and more deeply into technological-political *relationships)* the product is far greater uncertainty. Thus, it is better to develop techniques for the appropriate handling of uncertainty in making policy than to encourage and to lean upon random guesses.

ROBERT C. NORTH and NAZLI CHOUCRI

Population, Technology, and Resources in the Future International System

The population problems of the future are commonly discussed in terms of overcrowding and such basic needs as food, water, urban housing and services, and health. There is scattered evidence to suggest, however, that population levels and growth rates may also be important elements affecting war, peace, and man's patterns and styles of social, economic, and political organization.

Historians have frequently referred to population and its growth (or decline) as causes of great migrations, territorial expansions, wars, conquests, changes in the pattern or volume of trade, and industrial growth

Robert C. North is Professor of Political Science, and Director of Studies in International Conflict and Integration, Institute of Political Studies, at Stanford University. He is the author of *Moscow and Chinese Communists* and other books and articles concerned with international relations, international conflict, crises, and the antecedents of war.

Nazli Choucri is Assistant Professor of Political Science at M.I.T., and received the Ph.D., at Stanford University in 1967. Dr. Choucri's recent work includes articles on international alignments and non-alignment, empirical analyses of conflict and warfare, and a comparative assessment of forecasting methodologies. Dr. Choucri is co-author with Robert C. North of a forthcoming volume entitled *Nations in Conflict: Prelude to World War I.*

Prepared for delivery at the Sixty-sixth Annual Meeting of the American Political Science Association, Biltmore Hotel, Los Angeles, California, September 8-12, 1970.

(or stagnation). Few efforts have been made, however, to explain the causal connections in a consistent way or to develop a unified theory. This essay will suggest several of the ways in which world population levels and rates of growth may combine with other variables to influence future human institutions and behavior.

In an effort to meet their needs and demands, human beings use knowledge and skills in order to improve their access to resources. Toward this end they make tools and machines which may be viewed as auxiliaries to the human mind and body in the performance of certain functions, but these also require resources. Hence, the more advanced the level of technology among a given population, the greater is likely to be the range and quantity of resources needed to sustain and advance that technology. Advancing knowledge and skills also alter a people's perceptions of what they "need" and consequently their demands are likely to increase.

The application of knowledge and skills, like biological metabolism, depends upon complex energy transformation chains.[1] Each transformation of energy for such applications involves some amount of degradation from an available, concentrated form to an unavailable, dispersed form. During earlier stages of history and prehistory man could only gradually utilize energy-rich materials. Later, as his knowledge and skills increased, he learned to make increasingly complex alterations and transformations. He learned to unlock larger amounts of resources from the environment and to turn them to useful purposes.[2]

None of this transformed energy came free. At the very least a human being had to expend some amount of his own energy in order to obtain resources and extract a greater amount of food or mechanical energy from the environment. More complex transformations required the investment of considerable amounts of stored mechanical energy in order to generate larger amounts of applicable energy and to maintain it ready for use. Each transformation and application of energy thus tended to exact a toll upon the environment. For example, the excessive exploitation of a forest not only exhausted the local supply of trees, but also encouraged erosion and contributed to floods. In terms of human energy expended, materials consumed, wastes accumulated, and damaging side effects, some types of energy transformation were more costly than others. Over

[1] Howard T. Odum, *An Energy Circuit Language for Ecological and Social Systems: Its Physical Base.* Progress Report to the U.S. Atomic Energy Commission, Appendix 1, Based on Studies Supported by the U.S. Atomic Energy Commission of Biology and Medicine, Contract At-(40-1)-3666, November 1969.

[2] For a discussion of food chains, see Odum, "Energetics of World Food Production," *op.cit.*

much of human prehistory and history, however, the earth was so large and bountiful compared to the number of people and their resource requirements, that depletion and waste had only local significance.

In nation-states and empires, population and technology combine multiplicatively to produce human demands for resources. Such demands may be generated among the ruling elite or among the general populace or among both. They may be partially satisfied by the acquisition of resources either from original sources or through trade. Hence, the scarcer the resources relative to population and level of knowledge and skills, the greater will be the level of unsatisfied demands. This proposition can be broadly summarized in the following equation:

$$\frac{\text{Population X Technology (Knowledge and Skills)}}{\text{Resources (Ecology and Environment)}} = \text{Demands}$$

This formulation applies to a local situation or to a nation-state, an empire or to the whole world. Not only does technology create demands for resources, but advances in knowledge and skills also tend to increase the array of items which people *think* they need.

Over the course of man's prehistory and history certain processes of socio-cultural learning (together with increases in his numbers) have given rise to remarkable changes in his ways of living. These changes include not only the development of powerful tools, weapons, and machines capable of spectacularly altering the environment, but also the devising and operating of new methods of social, political, and economic organization. In general, the higher the level of socio-cultural learning (knowledge and skills) in a given society, the greater the advantage enjoyed by that society in gaining access to (or controlling) energy-rich substrates. Over long periods of time certain crude analogies are evident between organic evolution and socio-cultural "evolution." To the extent that technology develops in a given society, "an evolution in the direction of better fit to the selective system becomes inevitable."[3] The concept of "fit" should be viewed reciprocally, in terms of the environment fitting people just as much as people fitting the environment.[4]

Given a natural propensity for environmental change—alterations in the physical environment as well as in human environments with which a given human being or interpersonal organization is interacting—it is

[3] Joseph Needham, "Evolution," *Encyclopedia of the Social Sciences,* Vol. 5 (1957), p. 652.

[4] Donald T. Campbell, "Variation and Selective Retention in Socio-Cultural Evolution," *General Systems: Yearbook of the Society for General Systems Research,* Vol. XIV (1969), p. 73.

probable that eventually a previously adaptive pattern of behavior will cease to be adaptive. It will no longer "fit." We may expect, then, that ". . . at many levels of cultural development, and for organic evolution, variation is at the expense of jeopardizing the already achieved adaptive system." When appropriate learning and adaptation fail to take place in a given society, a severe strain is likely to be felt.[5]

The efforts of people over many millenia to organize in order to perform certain functions resulted in greater centralization of decision and control, a general increase in reliance upon coercive institutionalized sanctions, more reliance on technology, and a more complex division of labor. The emergence of the state as the virtually universal mechanism of organization, unification, and integration in human society represents a stage in socio-cultural evolution that is qualitatively different from earlier stages such as band, tribe or chiefdom. What, then, distinguishes a state? According to Elman Service, "A true state, however underdeveloped, is distinguishable from chiefdoms in particular and all lower levels in general by the presence of that special form of control, the consistent threat of force by a body of persons legitimately constituted to use it."[6] This decision and control apparatus—based upon a recognized, "legitimatized" monopoly of force which claims to oversee all other institutions within its boundaries—may be displayed in a variety of particular forms by quite disparate societies with small and large populations.

Much of the cohesion and effectiveness of a state also tends to emerge from the popular internalization of authority symbols, the sharing of values and expectations, the inculcation of loyalties and a sense of duty, and the concern of the head of state and the elite with mediation among components of the society, with the performance of ceremonial and often religious functions, and with the fulfillment of a variety of protective and even benevolent roles. National leaderships operate to minimize or close one (or a combination) of three types of gap. A gap between resources that are demanded or "needed" and resources that are actually available is the most basic.[7] The second is the gap between an expectation and the reality that materializes (as when climbing productivity begins to decline).[8] The third is a gap between the state's level of resources, growth

---

[5] *Ibid.*, p. 73.

[6] Elman R. Service, *Primitive Social Organization* (New York: Random House, 1962), p. 171.

[7] This concept can be broadened to include social demands or "needs" and other benefactions.

[8] Cf. Raymond Tanter and Manus Midlarsky, "A Theory of Revolution," *The Journal of Conflict Resolution,* Vol. XI, No. 3 (September 1967).

or production rate and that of a rival.[9] The behavior of a state at any given time may be understood largely by the existence of one or a combination of such gaps. Gaps in military and naval power, prestige, and status may exacerbate related resource gaps or create new ones.

The first gap involves biological necessities such as food, water, air, and some amount of territory. A people must have access, directly or through trade, to materials which provide the minimal energy they require for survival. Beyond this, the first gap involves the resources that are required for the application of their knowledge and skills, and also the resources that are demanded in order to supply them with whatever additional goods they think are immediately necessary. The second gap refers to expectations of future growth. Societies that have been achieving increments of growth year by year come to expect further increments in the future.[10] Hence, if the growth rate declines, national leaders and much of the populace may develop feelings of uneasiness, dissatisfaction, or frustration. The third gap emerges from situations of competition where one country begins to compare its capabilities and growth in agriculture, commerce, industry or military power with the capabilities and growth of another country. Absolute levels of population, technology, territory, resources, and trade affect a nation's overall capabilities, power, prestige, and status. Moreover, rates of change along these dimensions shape a nation's predispositions and behavior.

If a society's population is too large relative to its level of knowledge and skills, demands are likely to be high, but the people will in large part lack the capabilities to meet them. Such a society will confront difficulties in locating, extracting, and processing scarce resources. It may have difficulty in maintaining domestic communications, cohesion, order, and effectiveness. It will also be vulnerable to economic, political, and military penetration, exploitation, and domination by stronger powers. To maintain itself, the populace should be able to produce at a volume and rate considerably above its level and rate of consumption. Favorable trade can add to the level of available resources in the denominator of the demands equation, but a society cannot be really powerful unless the level of knowledge and skills is raised commensurately with the growing population.

In their efforts to close gaps between what is available and what is needed (or demanded), both individuals and interpersonal systems tend to

[9] Cf. Alan Howard and Robert A. Scott, "A Proposed Framework for the Analysis of Stress in the Human Organism," *Behavioral Science,* Vol. X, No. 2 (April 1965).
[10] Tanter and Midlarsky, *op.cit.*

allocate certain proportions of the resources available to them for the development of specific capabilities. These special capabilities may involve methods of hunting, trading, agriculture, warfare, and industrial production. The general nature of a society's institutions and government is likely to reflect the social requirements of the technology that prevails within it. Similarly, in modern cases, the distribution of the budget of a state or empire is a good indicator of the society's operational, as opposed to its professed, values.

Population, technology, territory-resources, and trade can be combined in the following ways to yield characteristic patterns and predispositions:

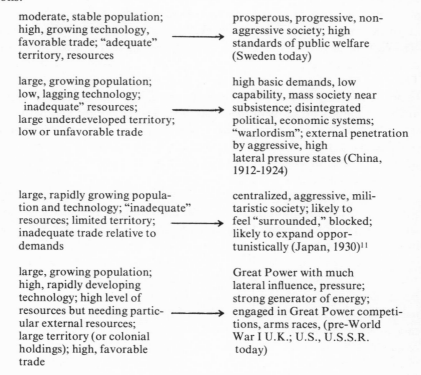

moderate, stable population; high, growing technology, favorable trade; "adequate" territory, resources ⟶ prosperous, progressive, non-aggressive society; high standards of public welfare (Sweden today)

large, growing population; low, lagging technology; inadequate" resources; large underdeveloped territory; low or unfavorable trade ⟶ high basic demands, low capability, mass society near subsistence; disintegrated political, economic systems; "warlordism"; external penetration by aggressive, high lateral pressure states (China, 1912-1924)

large, rapidly growing population and technology; "inadequate" resources; limited territory; inadequate trade relative to demands ⟶ centralized, aggressive, militaristic society; likely to feel "surrounded," blocked; likely to expand opportunistically (Japan, 1930)[11]

large, growing population; high, rapidly developing technology; high level of resources but needing particular external resources; large territory (or colonial holdings); high, favorable trade ⟶ Great Power with much lateral influence, pressure; strong generator of energy; engaged in Great Power competitions, arms races, (pre-World War I U.K.; U.S., U.S.S.R. today)

Some technologies have a high degradation/effectiveness ratio, that is, they render large amounts of energy non-available and useless or contaminating to life while "producing" relatively little. Their implications are entropic for the social system. Military applications tend to be especially illustrative. A major purpose of other applications—such as a water

---

[11] Japanese trade during the 1930's might be viewed as high, but insufficient for the rapidly increasing demand for resources.

filtration system—is to refurbish demands. The critical question is, does a particular application of technology refurbish sufficiently more than it "consumes" or degrades? The difficulty of the old dream of pumping water out of the ocean, desalinating it, lifting it over the mountains, and using it to make the Sahara Desert bloom involves the current high cost in terms of degradation for each unit of environmental (denominator) refurbishment.

This consideration raises difficult problems of means and ends. Means for achieving desirable ends differ substantially in their degradation/effectiveness ratios, some giving off much larger amounts of polluting effluents than others, and some "costing" the environment much less for each unit of benefit. What is a "benefit" on one dimension may not be on another, however. Thus, the manufacture and use of DDT eradicated malaria in many parts of the world, but had a "degrading" effect on a wide range of animal life via the food chain; and the application of bombs and defoliants to the Vietnamese countryside may be considered a "benefit" to U.S. foreign policy, but in ecological terms this use of technology adds up to almost utter degradation of energy, almost total "cost" and destructiveness. A waste water filtration plant, on the other hand, exacts some cost in degradation but yields vast amounts of cleaned, refurbished water—a vital resource to man and other forms of life.

As world population grows and technology advances, a major policy question *eventually* is going to be how to discourage applications of technology which severely degrade the denominator (ecology, resources) and develop other applications that meet demands at low cost to the environment. Clearly, this will involve a very considerable change in the nature of human demands.

There is another serious consideration, however. Up to now, much of the concern over population, ecology, and environment has focussed on (a) the problem of supplying adequate amounts of food; (b) ways to avoid depletion of other basic resources; (c) preservation of adequate living space; and (d) the control or elimination of certain types of pollution. We propose two further concerns that are interrelated and also of great importance for man's future: (e) the uneven access to basic resources of different societies and states; and (f) the contributions of differentials in population, technology, and access to resources to international conflict and violence (itself a great depletor of resources, especially in an era of defoliants and nuclear weaponry).

We have asserted that rising population, advancing technology, and "inadequate" or lagging access to resources create demands which a society then tries to meet by developing specialized capabilities. This also involves further considerations: the combination of demands and specialized capabilities (whether in agriculture, commerce, industry, military power) gives rise to what might be called lateral pressure. We use lateral pressure as a neutral term to express a society's tendency to exert efforts in one mode or another, or in a combination of modes, ever farther from its natural or original borders. This can occur as an attempt to meet demands for resources (and/or markets), or because a society has generated surplus capital for investment, or for other reasons. Lateral pressure may be generated in either public or private sectors and by "socialist" as well as "capitalist" states, and it can be expressed in terms of exploration, foreign trade, investment, conquest, acquisition of territory, domination over other societies, or even journeys to the moon. This concept can be expressed in an oversimplified way by the following formulation:

$$\text{Demands} \times \left\{ \begin{array}{c} \text{Specialized capabilities} \\ \text{in agriculture, commerce, industry,} \\ \text{investment, military power, etc.} \end{array} \right\} = \begin{array}{c} \text{Lateral} \\ \text{Pressure} \end{array}$$

Because they generate rapidly increasing needs and demands for resources and are also likely to produce highly specialized capabilities, a growing population combined with an advancing technology is likely to give rise to increasing lateral pressure expressed in one mode or another, and often even in a combination of different modes. During the late 19th and early 20th centuries, colonial expansion was a characteristic mode of lateral pressure by the Great Powers which thereby acquired vastly more than their proportionate shares of access to resources and markets.

Since World War II the possibilities for colonial expansion have been severely limited, and lateral pressure has been expressed much more in terms of trade and aid programs, military assistance to client countries, the establishment of bases, and the stationing of troops overseas. The size of the colonial population no longer serves as a viable indicator of the expansion of a country's interests. Control is frequently exerted now through a variety of means other than direct rule. Sometimes these influences are quite subtle. It has been argued that Great Powers tend to concentrate their trade with smaller states in an attempt to use commerce as an indirect means of control. Nazi Germany's harsh trade relations with the countries of Eastern Europe have been interpreted in this light.[12] Gen-

---

[12] Albert O. Hirschman, *National Power and the Structure of Foreign Trade* (Berkeley: University of California Press, 1945). It is not the *amount* of trade a small state devotes to a larger Power that is important in this respect, but rather the *proportion* of trade with the

erally it is the more technologically advanced polities that are capable of pressuring, influencing, and controlling less effective societies.

By yielding resources, trade has the possibility of alleviating demands (adding to the resource base of the society). A high lateral pressure country may in fact use trade as a means for dominating a low capability country, but this need not be so. Although there are undoubtedly numerous exceptions, the trend seems to be in the direction of high capability countries getting stronger and richer (and consuming a greater proportion of the world's resources) relative to the low capability countries. This trend is likely to become exacerbated as nuclear reactors and other tools of technology require larger and larger bases of specialized knowledge and skills.

Some countries have consciously developed commercial capabilities in preference to political expansion or coercion. In this respect the Scandinavian countries stand in sharp contrast to the Great Powers: commerce—not conquest, expansion, or warfare—has provided the dominant mode of external behavior. However conscious this decision may have been on the part of the national leadership, it is nonetheless a reality that these countries had neither the manpower nor the accompanying rate of growth that would sustain a more belligerent international posture. In 1960 the combined populations of the four Scandinavian countries amounted to approximately ten million less than the population of Great Britain one century earlier. Furthermore, rates of growth were almost one and a half times lower than those of Great Britain.

As a nation-state or empire extends influence (and hence its interests), a feeling frequently tends to develop among the elite (and often among the populace) that this influence and the expanding interests (whether public or private) ought to be protected. Where feasible, powerful states and empires tend also to inhibit their rivals or enemies from extending their interests into new territory. These tendencies may give rise to the extension of military or naval forces, the development of a tendency to police areas beyond the legal boundaries of the state or empire, and a feeling of responsibility for regional or even world "law and order."

During the 19th and early 20th century, Great Britain played such a role *par excellence,* and it was this British advantage that German leaders were increasingly inclined to challenge. Similarly, after World War I, an aspiring Japan (with her rapidly growing population and technology) saw Great Britain and the U.S. defending an advantageous status quo at her expense. With the disintegration of the British and French empires after

---

larger Power in relation to the total amount of trade undertaken by the smaller state that is an indication of the degree of penetration by the larger.

World War II, the U.S. came to occupy the position in the world which England had previously occupied, steadily assuming responsibility in the Far East, Indochina, the Middle East, and elsewhere for old British and French functions which it performed, frequently, in new styles and modes. The desire to achieve and maintain law and order (as defined by the national leadership) and protect national and private interests in far off places may lead to wars against indigenous tribes, chiefdoms, petty principalities or low capability states in an effort to attract, equip, and partially finance client chiefs, princes, warlords or other rulers or ruling groups.

The Roman Empire, the British and French Empires of the 19th century, the U.S., the U.S.S.R., and other powers have all displayed this tendency. Of the 21 wars between 1870 and 1914, each involving Richardson scale casualties between 3,000 and 31,000, almost all emerged from the extension or maintenance of colonial domain. Only three involved direct confrontation among the powers. More frequent were collisions between Great Powers and client states.[13] Since World War II client states have played a major role in the waging of cold wars. To the extent that two (or more) countries with high energy levels and high lateral pressure tendencies extend their interests and psycho-political borders outward, there is a strong probability that sooner or later the opposing perimeters of interest will intersect at one or more points. There is often a feeling on the part of an aspiring but weaker or less prestigious power that it is being "encircled" by its rivals. When this happens, competition will intensify and result in a conflict, "cold war," or an arms race. Crises are likely to emerge around such intersection points.

These tendencies often lead to wars between either the two or more high lateral pressure nations or their local clients or both. The French and Indian wars in North America (during which Algonquin tribes were clients of the French and Iroquois tribes were clients of the British) and French-English clashes in India (and clashes between British and French client rajahs and sultans) during the 18th century offer classic examples. More recently, the Vietnam War and the Middle East situation provide additional illustrations of these dynamics, complicated, of course, by the intricacies of local conflicts. That both the level and the rate of increase of the Egyptian population are so much higher than those of the Israeli population is undoubtedly a critical consideration in Israeli defense calculations—much in the same way, perhaps, as the vast technological su-

---

[13] Lewis F. Richardson, *Statistics of Deadly Quarrels* (Chicago: Quadrangle Books, 1960), pp. 52-69. These comparisons are made *only* on the basis of wars involving one or more of the Major Powers.

periority of Israel features prominently in Egypt's own military calculations. The Middle East situation provides one of the most clear-cut cases of the interdependence and extreme salience of population dynamics and technological advancement. In many ways these considerations set the parameters within which psychological, sociological, and political factors come into play. It is self-evident that Soviet and American involvement in the area raises the probability of a global conflagration. In many respects contemporary Indochina can be viewed as a locus of intersection of U.S., Soviet, and mainland Chinese interests, complicated by strong North Vietnamese (and some South Vietnamese) lateral pressure.

On a fundamental level (and ignoring cultural ties), Russia's support of Serbia in 1914 against pressures from Austria-Hungary can be assessed in terms of increasing militarism in Europe. Each Power predicated its own defense calculations on those of its "adversaries"—either perceived, potential, or actual—and any increase in one nation's defense budget was matched by a comparable, though by no means identical, increase in the defense budgets of its "adversaries." But such competition becomes salient only to the extent that basic differentials in population growth, technological advancement, and access to resources have already become considerable and are perceived as such by all sides.[14]

In sum, levels and rates of growth of population and technology have political as well as ecological and economic implications. Uneven rates of growth of these dimensions and grossly unequal access to resources (and uneven capabilities for processing and applying them) give rise to the political and economic (and sometimes the military) penetration of low capability societies by high capability countries, and to international competitions, conflicts, arms races, crises, and wars.

Differentials in world and regional consumption of fuel energy offer a rough indicator of the spread between high capability and low capability countries:

	Total Energy Consumption Per Capita 1951[15]	*Total Energy Consumption Per Capita 1967*[16]
World	1070	1647
North America	7486	9665
Western Europe	2092	3148
Caribbean America	507	998
Other America	372	618
Africa	203	285
Far East	151	378

[14] Kendall D. Moll, *The Influence of History Upon Seapower, 1865-1914* (Menlo Park, California: Stanford Research Institute, September 1968); Richard P. Lagerstrom and Robert

27

Some gains were thus made by the less industrial regions of the world, but they were not spectacular. In 1951 the world per capita level was 7 times the per capita level in the Far East, and the North American per capita level was nearly 50 times that of the Far East. By 1967, the world level was somewhat more than 4 times, and the North American level was a little less than 30 times, the Far Eastern level. If the world were forced to depend on fossil fuels as its primary source of industrial energy, there would be little probability of "significantly improving the standard of living by industrialization of the so-called underdeveloped regions of the world" or of maintaining, on an unequal basis, the activities of the highly industrialized areas "at anything like present levels for more than a few centuries." There are even possibilities that shortages might develop "before the end of the present century." The only remaining source of energy "that does have the proper magnitude and does lend itself to large industrial uses is nuclear."[17]

In many respects the industrial superpowers are like huge vacuum cleaners sucking up resources from all over the world in order to maintain productivity, military capabilities, and consumer demands. In 1960 with 6 per cent of the world's population, the U.S. consumed approximately 30 per cent of the world's total production of minerals at that time. If the whole world had been industrialized to the same level, the annual drain in 1960 would be about 5 times what it actually was. At current population, technological, and consumption growth rates in the U.S., northwestern Europe, the U.S.S.R., Japan, and a few other industrialized regions, there is likely to be sharper competition for resources over the next 50 years unless a more rational and just distribution can be achieved.[18]

We have emphasized that high capability, high lateral pressure powers, in expanding their interests, obviously often dominate less developed countries. Frequently there is a feeling that such interests ought to be de-

---

C. North, "An Anticipated Gap, Mathematical Model of International Dynamics," Institute of Political Studies, Stanford University, April 1969 (mimeo.); Nazli Choucri and William C. Mitchell, "Armaments Behavior Among Competing Nations Simulating the Naval Budgets of Major Powers: Europe, 1870-1914," Department of Political Science, Massachusetts Institute of Technology and University of Chicago, October 1969.

[15] United Nations Statistical Papers, *World Energy Supplies,* Series J, No. 3, 1955-1958, Table 1, pp. 3, 4.

[16] *Ibid.,* No. 12, 1964-67, Table 1, pp. 10, 11.

[17] *Energy Resources,* A Report to the Committee on Natural Resources, National Academy of Sciences, National Research Council, Washington, D.C., 1962, pp. 132-133. See also Palmer C. Putnam, *Energy in the Future* (Princeton: Van Nostrand, 1953).

[18] *Energy Resources, op.cit.,* pp. 131-132.

fended. We have also underscored the fact that when the perimeters of interest of two (or more) high capability powers *intersect,* confrontations may develop, and the two powers may see themselves as competitors for influence and control. Each is likely to do what it can to deny the other the access it would like to resources, markets, and political and economic control of the low capability region.

Until the 20th century the world was much larger, relative to the number of people, and many societies were buffered from each other by time and space. Now, increasingly, we live elbow to elbow, cheek to jowl. As national populations increase, and as the technological capabilities of a few Great Powers create new demands, current intersections are likely to become exacerbated in the future. With greater reliance on electrical energy generated by nuclear plants, and as transportation and communications are further improved, the location of highly developed technologies is less likely to be determined by the immediate availability of the necessary raw materials and more by the availability of appropriate knowledge and skills. A few Great Powers are likely to enjoy considerable advantage in the development of breeder reactors and other transformers of energy, whereas low capability countries may suffer. These considerations suggest the potential for an even more subtle type of domination by strong countries over weaker countries.

Beyond this, the influence of population, technology, and access to resources raises troublesome questions about the control of international conflicts and the avoidance of war. It suggests that mediation, conciliation, adjudication, the development of international law, and other alternatives to war are not in themselves likely to be sufficient for the preservation of peace. On the contrary, the basic "causes" of war seem to reside in the uneven development of national dimensions and attributes over which, in the past, national and international political processes have had very little control. One might conjure up a somewhat oversimplified picture of a dozen nuclear missile establishments zeroed in on each other with the trip wires attached to a multivariate threshold involving differentials of population, technology, and access to resources and markets. This suggests the need for a. whole new set of worldwide investigations into the nature of these inequalities and uneven distributions of resources and capabilities. It suggests that the environment, resource allocation, the characteristics of different ecologies, and the "sovereign" state as a basic unit of political and economic organization are important starting places for research not only into the causes of war, but also for designing and putting into effect a more peaceful and effective alternative international system.

It suggests the encouragement of "social learning" and "social invention" to ensure a better "fit" between mankind and his environment—with attention to the interests and integrity of the individual.

These observations raise the question of whether ways can be found to guarantee low capability countries a fair share not only of food and other basic resources, but also of access to nuclear and other energy transferring modes free of Great Power control, domination, competitions, and conflicts. This also requires access to related communication and transportation facilities. It points toward the development and control of such technological complexes by international public agencies through which low capability countries of the world are enabled to participate and maintain their rightful shares of decision and control.

Closely associated with this is the need for continuing research into the social, economic, and political "costs" of new technologies as well as into their more narrowly and technically defined effectiveness and efficiency. For each unit of output, how costly is a given technology in terms of depleting the resources denominator of the demands equation and in terms of damage to the quality of human living? Some application of knowledge and skills—for which DDT might become a model—may imply both gains and losses to human life on the planet. In even more fundamental terms, modern military establishments should come under close scrutiny with respect to their effects on the environment and on future human life as a whole—in addition to their immediate casualty-producing implications.

All these considerations have implications for conservatives, liberals, and radicals alike. Preservation of the status quo is likely to lead to a series of disasters; reliance on "good will," exhortation, and "faith in mankind" is not likely, in itself, to move men to make the changes that are required; and the substitution of a new elite, a new ideology, or a new political system will also be useless in the long run unless careful provision is made for investigation into these deep, underlying problems and for the identification and carrying out of alternatives that will ameliorate problems which, so far, virtually no ideology or political system has taken into sufficient account. First, the most pressing needs are to identify (and develop) promising organizational, procedural, and technical alternatives and second, to employ our pedagogical and communications skills to educate the people of the world about the crucial tasks that lie ahead.

HERBERT S. DINERSTEIN

The Future of Ideology
in Alliance Systems

I. *Introduction*

This article investigates the future role of ideology in alliances by comparing its role in the 16th and 17th centuries, when both Protestantism
and nationalism emerged to challenge older beliefs, with its role in the
post-1917 period. The comparison seeks to suggest what remains constant
and what varies in the relationship between ideology and alliances. Comparisons with the ideological impact of the French Revolution on alliances and the Greek-Spartan conflict in the 5th century, B.C., would
probably have been quite helpful, but time and space were lacking.

Ideology is both normative and analytical. The term was first used
pejoratively in the early 19th century to characterize those Frenchmen
who wanted to guide the politics of the Napoleonic state by the abstract
principles of the French Revolution. Later in the century it lost its negative connotation, and now Communists and non-Communists employ the

Herbert S. Dinerstein is Professor of Soviet Studies at The Johns Hopkins School of Advanced International Studies and an associate of the Washington Center of Foreign
Policy Research. He was educated in New York City public schools and Harvard University. After service with the Office of War Information, he taught and until 1966 was a
member of The RAND Corporation. He has published on Soviet agricultural, military,
and foreign policies and is now working on Soviet policy in Latin America.

Prepared for delivery at the Sixty-sixth Annual Meeting of the American Political Science Association, Biltmore Hotel, Los Angeles, California, September 8-12, 1970. Copy-
right, 1970, The American Political Science Association.

term to explain large and complex social phenomena. The Soviet definition emphasizes the class, transnational character of ideology. Non-Communists also accepted the universal character of socialist ideology, especially before the appearance of heresies within the socialist movement. Non-socialist analysts have at times spoken in terms of national ideologies, but have hardly ever ascribed an ideology to a group smaller than a nation.

II. *Revolutionary and Counter-Revolutionary Ideologies*

Protestantism. At first neither Protestants nor their opponents believed that they were revolutionaries. Both John Huss and Martin Luther claimed to have come to reform the Church and to save it from itself just as Jesus claimed to have come to save and purify Judaism. But Lutheranism quickly passed beyond reformism. The support offered by the German princes who wanted to assert their independence from the Holy Roman Emperor and the Papacy pushed Lutheranism toward the denial of the papal monopoly of authority in Christian doctrine. Lutheranism assumed that there was a single religious truth that the political authority should enforce. But it ultimately furthered the development of national authorities with differing religious beliefs, who insisted on uniformity of faith among their subjects. While Luther was reluctant to create a rival center of religious authority, Calvin made no attempt to win Rome over, asserting his own authority instead. The Anabaptists and the more radical sects, based on the poorer classes who had rarely appeared on the stage of history, tended to deny not only the authority of Rome, but also the right of secular authority to determine religious doctrine. This extreme wing of Protestantism never achieved enough power to influence diplomatic alignments in a significant way.

Although Lutheranism and English Protestantism in their early stages were unaware that they had broken the unity of the faith, they became self-conscious proponents of a new view of the world.

Nationalism. The idea of the nation preceded the first successful establishment of Protestantism and then developed together with it. By the 20th century the ideology of nationalism, often called *raison d'état* or the doctrine of national interest, had become the antithesis of ideology. In the late 15th century in Italy and in the 16th century in other Western European countries, however, the notion of the supremacy of state interests, with only summary or no reference to the restrictive action of the law of God or of natural law, was a revolutionary idea.

The shift from dynastic and feudal to state interests reflected a military and economic revolution. The improvement in sources of revenue, communications, and administrative apparatus made possible and then necessary the replacement of short-term recruits from the nobility with mercenary troops requiring extensive training first in the use of the pike and later the musket. In the 15th century the Italian city-state was about the maximum size for such an administrative military apparatus depending on mercenary troops. In the 16th century with the slow but steady improvement in communications, larger units, notably Spain and France, could wage up-to-date warfare. The national state could better challenge the Papacy than the kings of earlier centuries. Not that these kings had hesitated to humble the Pope and force his hand, but they lacked the will and power to maintain a sustained anti-Roman policy. Hence, the consolidation of power within the new nation-state made an independent religious policy possible. The state could now wage longer wars without inducing the nobility to fight at their own expense and, somewhat later, without special war taxes on the towns. The longer wars were more destructive than the wars of the Italian Renaissance states only a century earlier when the mercenaries, confronted by a superior force, would often negotiate a settlement to avoid a mutually destructive battle. In the next century when the warmakers were richer and were driven by ideological passion, the destructiveness of war mounted, reaching an apogee during the Thirty Years War.

Socialism. After 1917 the revolutionary ideology of socialism was joined to a state, albeit a battered state, to become a vigorous proselytizing ideology. To its adherents the Marxist ideology was based on science, not faith; to its opponents it seemed more like scientism than science. It bridged the philosophical dilemma of choice between free will and predestination by arguing analytically that capitalism and the imperialist system were foreordained to collapse, but insisting, normatively, that socialists had to struggle to hasten that day. Very soon the national interests of the first socialist state prevailed over its proselytizing penchant on the ground that the preservation of the first socialist state and the interests of world socialism were identical. Nothing in Soviet ideology militated against alliances with capitalist countries and such alliances were a feature of the inter-war system. In the post-war period, however, when the ideological tension between the two camps sharpened and the hegemonial power in each camp was very much stronger than the next largest power, formal alliances between communist and non-communist states were not contemplated.

33

Heretical revolutionary ideology. Within Protestantism, since Lutheranism and Calvinism emerged almost simultaneously, it was difficult to say which of the two represented heresy to the new faith. The Lutherans and Calvinists were often as hostile to each other as the Russians and the Chinese are now. The U.S.S.R. with its undisputed claim to priority presumes to define heresy. Thus far the Chinese Communists, the Yugoslavs, the Albanians, and the Dubcek Communists have earned this designation. They have returned the compliment by charging that the U.S.S.R. represents a degeneration of socialism. However reluctantly, the Protestants had to accommodate diversity among themselves from the outset. For the U.S.S.R. different "Communisms" came as a shock and much energy has been expended in the effort to attain ideological unity. Heretical revolutionary ideology has affected alliance systems because of its legitimizing function.

Counter-revolutionary ideology. As the revolutionary ideology gathers momentum and appears to represent the "wave of the future," it provokes a counter-revolution that can either reform the abuses that provoked the new revolutionary ideology or try to regain lost ground by a militant program. Erasmus and his followers represented the first approach as did the Jesuits and the Capuchins in the early phase of their activities, although later these orders became the cutting edge of the militant Counter Reformation. The anti-Communism of the 20th century was not as single-minded as the Counter Reformation. The anti-communist camp could not offer an unambiguous doctrinal profile, since the democratic states have never been very self-conscious about their ideology and have never felt the necessity for promulgating an official credo. After World War II the anti-communist camp was satisfied with containment rather than reconquest in contrast to the Catholic Counter Reformation. To the extent that counter-revolutionary ideologies are highly self-conscious, they perform a legitimizing function.

III.   *The Development and Structure of Ideological Groupings*

The way in which ideological alliance systems were formed has naturally affected their character. The Protestant system developed very slowly—a circumstance which contributed to its stability. The new Protestant states enjoyed a long respite before they had to face the onslaught of the Counter Reformation. The old struggle between Pope and Emperor and the dynastic struggles in Europe had a higher priority than the Protestant threat.

   For the Pope, as an Italian prince, the overriding issue was the Spanish control of Milan and Naples. The Pope's first priority was to reduce and eliminate the Spanish presence in Italy. The natural ally in this endeavor was France, which was "encircled" by the Spanish. Due to an accident of dynastic inheritance, the Dukes of Burgundy, who also had extensive holdings in the Netherlands, were Hapsburgs and Charles V had inherited both the Spanish and Austrian thrones. Francis I sought to break out of this vise by an alliance with the Turkish Sultan Suleiman and by various arrangements with the German Protestants. In a sense the Papacy by its pro-French policy was indirectly supporting the Moslems and the Protestants. The felt necessity to temporize and the concomitant unwillingness to make doctrinal accommodations gave Protestantism a breathing space in which to develop. For his part Charles V was also inclined to postpone the confrontation, first because he hoped for compromise, and second because he needed the votes of the Protestant princes in the Holy Roman Empire to confirm his brother Ferdinand of Austria as the King of Rome which made him the Emperor designate.

The U.S.S.R. obtained its period of respite partially because of divisions among its opponents and partially because its very weakness seemed to make it safe to temporize. In the interwar period the conflicts among the non-socialist states inhibited whatever ideological impulse to intervene persisted after the failure of the 1917-1921 armed intervention. After the war the overwhelming industrial and nuclear superiority of the U.S., the weariness of Europe's people, and the American distaste for a new war, a sentiment also prevalent among those disposed to take the threat of communist ideology most seriously, combined to give the U.S.S.R. time to consolidate control in the new socialist states. By the time sentiment had shifted, the U.S.S.R. had acquired new strength and the desirability of "rolling Communism back" had to be weighed against very extensive risks.

In the 16th and 17th centuries Protestantism and nationalism developed simultaneously. By the end of the 17th century it was quite clear, however, that the dominant influence on the international system had been nationalism and that the influence of religion had been a transient phenomenon. In the 20th century, by contrast, the first socialist state was as self-conscious about the novelty of its ideology as were its opponents. Few doubted that the socialism of the U.S.S.R. represented a sharp break with the past, whereas from the first the Protestant states were enmeshed in the European diplomatic system. Despite the different levels of participation in the international system, actors in the two periods shared the conviction that conflict was inevitable. As the understanding spread that Protestantism indeed represented something new, arrangements between

Protestant and Catholic rulers were viewed as temporary truces, to be followed by renewed fighting until one finally destroyed the other. The Soviet leaders and their opponents viewed cross-ideological alliances in much the same way. Only the realization of the destructiveness of nuclear war forced the U.S.S.R. in 1956 formally to adopt the doctrine of the necessity of peaceful coexistence. This doctrine effectively retired the idea that one side must triumph completely. In the U.S. the same necessity was accepted with less violence to ideological tenets and hence without formal promulgation.

The U.S.S.R. was weaker than most of the capitalist states and to the imbalance in economic and military strength was added the relative backwardness of the socialist states. The Catholic system contained the two most modern states, France and Spain, together with some more traditional states in the East. The U.S.S.R. was weaker than a number of capitalist states before World War II, and the new states in the socialist system after 1944 contained very few modern states. Czechoslovakia was the only exception and by the early 1960's it had slipped into the ranks of backward states. The relative economic and military weakness of the socialist states has much influenced their foreign policy. Although communist *movements* have often been willing to take risks to seize power, as in China and Indochina, socialist states have avoided military confrontations with superior non-socialist states. Thus, the U.S.S.R. has never engaged the U.S. in hostilities, and in its only conflict since 1921 with a great power, Germany, it was attacked. The Chinese only engaged the U.S. in hostilities when the Americans changed their war aims in Korea from the restoration of a *status quo ante* to unification.

By the 16th and 17th centuries the presumed ideological leader, the Papacy, had been discredited by the Babylonian Captivity (in Avignon) and the almost completely secular interests of the Renaissance Popes. The natural secular candidates for leadership of the anti-Protestant alliance system, first the Spanish Hapsburgs and then the Austrian Hapsburgs, suffered from several disabilities. The Spanish monarchs suffered from the almost permanent hostility of the French and the British. Furthermore, the expulsion of some Jews and the persecution of others who had adopted Christianity inhibited the replacement and growth of the commercial classes which furnished a modern state with the sinews of war. The Austrian Hapsburgs could never sustain a long-term campaign against the German princes because their energies were deflected from time to time by Ottoman advances which twice threatened the city of Vienna itself.

Paradoxically, the very great military and economic superiority of the

20th century counter-revolutionary system contained within it an element of advantage for its opponents. Even during the short period when some in the West believed that the two systems were intrinsically inimical, the confidence in superiority permitted the acceptance of a policy of containment, that is, holding the line in the belief that the basic weaknesses of the other system would cause it to collapse from within. Quite soon this most sanguine expectation gave way to an acceptance of the already existing socialist states and a determination to prevent an increase in their number. This U.S. self-limitation of its goals was neither precisely articulated nor consistently applied, but its significance was sufficiently appreciated in the socialist camp to make heresy appear safe. The appearance of communist heresies was perhaps inevitable, but the effective U.S. abandonment of the goal of "roll-back" made the socialist world safe for diversity. As communist confidence in U.S. restraint was reinforced by the development of first Soviet and then Chinese deterrents, the hostility among the communist states found rapid and virulent expression.

IV. *The Function of Ideology*

Rationalization. Perhaps ideology is most commonly employed within the socialist system to rationalize actions and decisions which might be made on other grounds. This is a common function of ideology and a few familiar examples are offered as illustrations. In the 17th century Cardinal Richelieu suppressed the Huguenots in the name of orthodoxy, but the real reason was the Huguenots' threat to the consolidation of royal authority. The Huguenots drew support from those of the nobility who feared the development of absolutism and from the townspeople who wanted to preserve their special status. Richelieu's motives are not far to seek, but reigning beliefs made it useful to cloak them in the mantle of religious orthodoxy. In Spain the official rationale for the Office of the Inquisition was the necessity to extirpate heresy. In fact, however, both the Papacy and the Spanish states and estates were denied the power of making appointments to the Holy Office, thus making the Inquisition an instrument for the consolidation of royal authority over internal and external rivals. A contemporary example is U.S. support for certain Latin American regimes through the Alliance for Progress on the rationale of general U.S. devotion to progress. But since dollars did not follow this devotion when the major communist threat was believed to lie in Europe and Asia, one is justified in designating this as a rationalization. The U.S.S.R. justified its support for Prime Minister Nasser of Egypt on the ground that he was a progressive force in the Arab world and incipiently socialist. But this too seems to be a rationalization for actions taken out of motives of traditional rivalry among states.

Legitimization. Although most Soviet foreign policy actions in any period are explicable in terms of a particular crisis, or of the desire to aggrandize power and influence, some foreign policy actions seem to derive from ideological needs. Particularly in socialist states, ideology serves a legitimizing function. An early example of legitimization is the Protestant policy of Elizabeth I of England. She had to define England as Protestant to establish herself as the legitimate ruler. The Protestant ideology legitimized her claim; Catholicism legitimized the claim of her half-sister, Mary, Queen of Scots. The Hapsburg Charles V was hardly a Catholic zealot or ideologue and not particularly noted for his attachment to his middle-aged aunt, Catherine (whose failure to produce a son made her divorce seem a necessity to Henry VIII). But an older system of beliefs, that of dynastic solidarity, made it impossible for him to pursue the policy of a British alliance against France which would have been most natural in pure power political terms.

William the Silent's religious journeys offer another case. Although William was born a German Lutheran, his parents had him raised as a Catholic when, at the age of 11, an unexpected series of deaths made him the heir to lands held by a Catholic prince. The older dynastic system, which persisted long after the beginning of the Protestant and national revolutions, made it possible for this German Lutheran prince to become a major vassal of Philip II of Spain. When Philip II of Spain tried simultaneously to suppress the ancient liberties of the Netherlands, rooted in medieval local privileges, and Protestantism, William the Silent assumed the leadership of the Netherlanders against Philip II. Although Lutherans and Calvinists combined were a minority compared to the Catholics, they in particular actively opposed Spanish rule, and once William the Silent decided that the Spanish rule had made itself intolerable by its repressive efforts, he found it necessary to legitimize his leadership of the revolt and his position with the activist minority of the population by resuming the practice of Lutheranism, first quietly at home and then publicly.

In the U.S.S.R. the legitimization of the regime is a continuing necessity. Although the U.S.S.R. has been in existence for 50 years, has made excellent economic progress in absolute terms, and has proceeded from a position of semi-backwardness to modernity, its regime still needs to be legitimized. The reasons are well known and need be referred to only briefly.[1] Socialism is appropriately classed as a materialist ideology because the rewards promised to its adherents are material rather than spiritual. Thus, there exists an objective standard by which to judge the success of the system. On the whole, Soviet citizens feel that the state has not fulfilled its promise of creature comforts and a decent standard of living. Now that 25 years have elapsed since the end of World War II, the argument that the destruction of war interfered with what would have been the normal progress of socialism is no longer convincing. Soviet citizens are aware that Japan, a country also devastated by war, has made enormous economic progress.

Second, the political arrangements in the U.S.S.R. are still constitutionally imperfect. The procedure for the replacement of the First Secretary of the Communist Party is not fixed. Each First Secretary has replaced his predecessor in a different manner, developed *ad hoc*. Thus, few within the U.S.S.R. know precisely how Khrushchev deposed Malenkov or how Khrushchev himself was deposed, and a wisp of mystery still surrounds the death of Stalin. These uncertain arrangements for succession inhibit the efficient conduct of state business since no incumbent knows the length of his term of office. Consequently, tentativeness and a constant search for political allies characterize the conduct of even those who remain in office for long periods. Demoralization is compounded by the circumstance that new incumbents to the first position make promises to abandon some of the hated policies of their predecessors and denounce them so violently that they are thus debarred from emulating those policies. Thus, to demonstrate that he would not restore the mass purges and the concentration camps, Khrushchev found it necessary to characterize Stalin as a criminal and demented in the last years of his life. Consequently, the official indoctrination of Soviet children can boast only two positive leaders, Lenin and the incumbent. It is as if American school children learned that the only good Presidents were George Washington and the incumbent and all the rest were Andrew Johnsons and Warren Hardings. This atmosphere of disappointment in the material accomplishments of the regime and the lack of genuine regard for the heads of the Party make it peculiarly necessary for Soviet political leaders to seek to legitimize the regime. Much the same considerations exist in most socialist countries.

An obvious source of legitimization is the socialism of the country. Although in the U.S.S.R. respect and regard for the persons of the ruling

[1] See my *Fifty Years of Soviet Foreign Policy* (Baltimore: The Johns Hopkins Press, 1968), pp. 34 ff.

group are not very widespread, the validity of socialism is generally accepted. Most Soviet citizens, even those hostile to the regime, believe that socialism is better than capitalism, that planned economies are better than unplanned, and they accept, in varying degrees, the proposition that a socialist regime must be supported because it is potentially, if not actually, the savior of mankind. Therefore, as long as the Soviet leaders can maintain that socialism is potentially a universal system with superior moral attributes, it can command a measure of support.

Relations with capitalist countries hardly touch the legitimacy of socialist regimes. Alliances with capitalist countries before 1941 could be satisfactorily explained as the skillful exploitation of differences among enemies; the wartime alliance with the U.S. and Great Britain was similarly justified. Limited cooperation with the U.S. after Stalin's death is convincingly explained as a necessity of the nuclear age.

By contrast, the legitimacy of the U.S.S.R. is challenged by socialist heresies. Precisely because socialism represents itself as an incipient universal system, bitter conflict among socialists (and ideological conflicts are always bitter) puts the whole ideology into question.

Disagreements with other socialist states feed back into the U.S.S.R. and bring to a critical point long smoldering domestic conflicts. For example, the ideological differences with Czechoslovakia in the spring and early summer of 1968 had concrete consequences for the U.S.S.R. Czechoslovakia, by propounding the slogan of "Communism with a human face," implied that the Soviet face of Communism was something less than human.[2] For example, the Czechoslovak experiment suspended the exercise of press censorship and thus furnished a striking and subversive contrast with Soviet practice; the nationalities in the multinational Czechoslovak People's Republic received a much more genuine form of federalism than any Soviet republic enjoys. The plans for economic liberalization if successfully executed would have deprived the Communist Party of Czechoslovakia of one of its major functions, since to decentralize economic decision-making is to reduce a vital function of communist parties. What is more, the prospective economic and political support from West Germany threatened to isolate and weaken the bargaining position of East Germany. The consequences might have been a political deterioration in that country with chain effects elsewhere.

These changes had almost immediate consequences in the U.S.S.R. Soviet intellectuals protested more boldly. The restoration of old privi-

---

[2] Zvi Y. Gitelman's unpublished paper, *The Diffusion of Political Innovation from Eastern Europe to the Soviet Union*, 1970.

leges to the small Ukranian minority in Czechoslovakia, particularly the permission granted the Uniate Church to resume its association with Rome rather than with the Patriarch in Moscow, was noted in the Soviet Ukraine and contributed to the crisis within the Ukrainian Communist Party. In general Soviet options in many areas and especially in economic planning would have been much reduced if the Czech economic reform had been successful. Soviet leaders feel with considerable justification that in a system so centrally directed and planned, mistakes can be particularly disastrous because they touch on so many aspects of society. Hence, they make changes very cautiously. The success of the Czechoslovak experiment would have put great pressures on a leadership committed to conservatism. For this reason alone Soviet leaders consider it necessary to impose ideological conformity, very narrowly defined, upon their allies. Heresy within the U.S.S.R. or within the socialist system is no more tolerable than was the propagation of Erasmian doctrines in Spain and Italy after the first notable successes of the Lutherans and Calvinists.

The conflict with China has been particularly difficult because the Soviet leaders cannot force their views on China. Because the levels of Soviet and Chinese economic, social, and educational development are so disparate, failure to agree on common goals was perhaps inevitable, but the disagreement was hastened and intensified by several circumstances. We have already referred to the assurance furnished by the realization that U.S. goals did not extend to "roll-back." In the Taiwan Straits crisis of 1958, the Chinese learned from their own experience that self-restraint was the key to avoiding a U.S. attack. The pursuit of intra-socialist differences no longer seemed to involve a temptation to a U.S. alert for an opportunity to initiate hostilities. Second, the U.S.S.R. tended to bargain with China in the style reserved for dealing with domestic insubordination. If a Soviet citizen ignores a warning, sanctions are exercised. With the increase in the severity of the sanctions, compliance usually follows and only rarely do principled oppositionists continue resistance at all costs. The Chinese, the Soviets were to realize, could not be credibly threatened with the international equivalent of the deprivation of liberty, and as the Soviets withdrew one after another of the benefits which made the alliance worthwhile to the Chinese, no further sanctions were available. The Soviets had made the egregious error of leaving nothing to deprive the Chinese of. Finally, the Soviet practice, emulated by the Chinese at the first opportunity, of intervening in factional fights and threatening particular leaders with loss of office, further embittered relations.[3]

---

[3] For a fuller treatment see my "The Soviet Union and China" in *Conflict in World Politics* edited by Steven L. Speigel and Kenneth N. Waltz (Cambridge, 1971).

The connection between legitimacy at home and the unity of the communist movement often makes Soviet relations with its allies and non-ruling parties the first priority. This often impedes diplomatic initiatives which offer a promise of success. For example, most agree that the division of Germany and the status of Berlin are the outstanding issues dividing the two ideological camps in Europe. Since the advent of the Kiesinger coalition government in 1966, and even more since the accession of the Social Democrat, Willy Brandt, to the Premiership, the West Germans have relaxed their opposition to an agreement on the "interim" division of Germany and formal recognition of the loss of German territory to Poland and the U.S.S.R. The Soviet opposition to exploring the West German initiatives was based on fear of adverse political consequences for the foreign and *internal* policies of socialist countries. The East German regime of Walter Ulbricht, despite marked improvements in economic production, feared the political consequences of the internal relaxation which would be demanded after some form of recognition from West Germany. After all, the ghost of revenge-seeking Germany would have been laid.

Until 1969 Gomulka was unwilling to accept West German recognition of the Oder-Neisse line and since 1956 Poland has continued to add conditions necessary to its acceptance of West German recognition of its new territories. Gomulka's change of heart was connected with an internal factional fight with General Moczar which Gomulka finally won. The U.S.S.R. was reluctant to press Gomulka to accept the West German overtures, because he loyally supported the U.S.S.R. at international communist meetings, and it seemed as if a Moczar victory would have challenged Soviet authority.

These rather obscure political fights illustrate how the Soviet need to present itself as the leader of a united communist movement delays a major step in the replacement of the cold war in Europe by an agreement to accept the status quo. The needs for internal legitimization thus deprive the U.S.S.R. of the opportunity to pursue favorable openings vigorously. Another consequence of preoccupation with ideology and legitimacy has been the need to repress internal dissidence, actually or potentially associated with an alien ideology. The pressure for internal uniformity is common to both periods under examination, but its intensity has varied.

In the 16th century Erasmianism had a wide vogue in Spain and in Italy and the prospects for the reform movement in the former country seemed particularly good. In few other countries was religion taken less for granted. The ethos of the Spanish nobility had been formed in the long struggle against Moslem rule and more than any other European monarch, the Spanish king felt himself to be the defender of a faith endangered by secret Moslems (Moriscos), secret Jews (Maranos), and finally, potential Protestants. Hence, when the Lutherans began to enjoy success in Europe, the reformists in Spain (and Italy) were harshly repressed. The most militant Counter Reformation order, that of the Jesuits, was founded by a Spaniard, Ignatius Loyola. Ideological purity was so important that a person suspected of heresy had to fear an investigation so severe that he might confess to a heresy he had never entertained. There were cases of defection from one side to another, the most famous being that of the Vicar General of the Capuchin order, Fra Bernadino da Siena who preached reform effectively and won many back to the old faith, until just before he fled over the Alps to join the Calvinists in Geneva.[4]

In the 20th century the counter-revolutionary ideological system has been less consistent in enforcing ideological purity. Although the Communist Parties of Greece, Spain, and Portugal are proscribed, the West German Communist Party (only recently permitted to function), the U.S. Communist Party (virtually proscribed until recently), and the large French and Italian Parties have remained legal. In the latter cases these Parties adopted a low posture. The French Communists permitted the forces of the Resistance, in which they exercised great influence, to be disarmed and absorbed into General de Gaulle's armies without a struggle; they also voted credits for the war in Indochina and muted their opposition to the war in Algeria until French opinion had shifted decisively. In Italy the Communist Party began its post-war career by agreeing to the continuation of Mussolini's Concordat of 1929 with the Vatican. With this first step the Italian Communist Party clearly established itself as a normal feature of the Italian political scene. As the ruling groups in France and Italy became convinced of the domestication of their own Communist Parties, the terrible struggle within the communist movements against heresy made the whole system seem less dangerous and reinforced confidence in the wisdom of tolerating communist parties.

In the several alliance systems in each of which the U.S. is the hegemon, political diversity rather than uniformity is the rule. Even in the most coherent of the alliances, NATO, several states neither claim nor would wish to claim that they are democratic. Others have a moderate form of state socialism. In the Asian and Latin American alliance systems, most states are not democratic; "free world" is obviously a euphemism for anti-Communism. Alliances with various non-democratic states hardly threaten the legitimacy of the governments of the U.S. or

---

[4] Father Cuthbert, *The Capuchins* (London: Sheed & Ward, 1928), Vol. 1, Chapter IV.

Great Britain, and although the U.S. might suffer some embarrassment over a reactionary regime in Greece, it hardly can be compared to the acute discomfort that regime changes within the socialist system cause the U.S.S.R.

The consolidation of communist power on the Chinese mainland, the various stages of the communist conquest of Indochina, and Castro's conversion to Communism have been more a political embarrassment to the incumbent American government than a threat to its legitimacy. Although U.S. political leaders voiced their anti-Communism with regularity, Republican Congressional leaders, until the outbreak of the Korean War in June 1950, were reluctant to vote the funds required to meet the dire threat described in their ideological preachments. Moreover, the Democrats' defeat in 1952 derived partially from their engagement in a war—against communist expansion. These circumstances suggest that anti-Communism served more as a rationalizing rather than a legitimizing function and that the accusation "soft on Communism" was most useful as a weapon of the outs against the ins. But to suggest that anti-Communism was a weapon in political infighting is not to suggest its unimportance. Domestically, President Kennedy believed that the Cuban conversion to Communism was politically costly to him. According to a sympathetic biographer, this belief contributed to his decision in 1961 to raise the level of involvement in Vietnam. Thus, in the early 1960's failure to pursue a successful policy of holding the line against Communism *anywhere* in the world was presumed to be expensive in terms of domestic political position.

Toward the middle 1960's, however, as the disintegrative effect of the internecine communist struggle began to be appreciated, the felt necessity for holding the line against Communism declined. If this last statement is valid, and there is much evidence to suggest that it is, the necessity arises for explaining the dogged continuance of the U.S. in a war in Vietnam at ever mounting political and economic costs. We shall defer consideration of this subject until we examine the shift from a conviction that conflict is to the death to the toleration of competing ideologies.

V. *The Effect of Ideology on Alliance Systems*

The perception of reality. At best the perception of reality by international actors is imperfect. On the eve of World War I, statesmen shared a basic understanding of the international system, and ideology had not yet formed prisms through which they viewed the world. Yet massive distortions of reality took place. One of the themes of a series of essays on the period[5] makes the point repeatedly that reality was misperceived. Delcassé, who was the Foreign Minister of France during the critical period, 1898-1905, believed without much foundation that Germany was actively seeking to gain a port on the Adriatic coast; this misperception helps explain his Anglophile and Russophile policies. Similarly, the British anticipated the German naval building program and took action which precipitated the development they had falsely predicted. Apprehension was the father of the self-fulfilling prophecy even in a period when ideology was not a distortant.

The historical accounts of the 16th and 17th centuries suggest that rulers then had better information than rulers now. Although communications were slow, typewriters and reproducing machines did not exist, and coding was clumsy, there were offsetting advantages. The political class and the group of decision makers was small and readily accessible. A good ambassador and a reasonably intelligent and diligent monarch could form a team for information acquisition and decision-making which modern governments could well envy. "Intelligence analysis" was easier in the 16th and 17th centuries than in the 20th. First, the number of international actors has increased and almost anyone can precipitate a crisis involving the great powers. By contrast, on the eve of the Thirty Years War, the issues which could lead to a general diplomatic crisis and to a war were fewer and well-known. All closely watched the political situation in the Swiss Grisons and the Val Telline because this mountain pass was used for the movement of the Spanish king's Italian mercenaries to the war in the Netherlands. The disposition of these few Swiss to permit or prevent passage of troops was critical. In the modern world it was difficult to predict that a serious crisis would erupt over the Congo or that the behavior of a misleadingly familiar caudillo in Cuba in 1957 and 1958 would in five short years lead to a nuclear confrontation between the U.S. and the U.S.S.R. Despite the enormous complexity and antiquity of the political structure of Europe in the 16th and 17th centuries, the basic elements were easier to distinguish and their interaction easier to comprehend than in the present.

Analysis has been further burdened by the increase in the number of domestic determinants of foreign policy. The ideological passions of the 16th and 17th centuries had indeed introduced a new dimension into the formation of national foreign policies. Some of the many examples can be cited. The extreme Protestants in Holland and Zealand (to whom the

---

[5] Walter Laqueur and George L. Mosse, editors, *1914: The Coming of the First World War* (New York: Harper Torch Books, 1966).

rivers and inland seas gave physical security against the armies of Spain) could not be conquered, and William the Silent was constrained to adopt their political and religious positions, which were more radical than he preferred. The French nobility, opposed to the consolidation of royal power, sought to enhance their power by becoming Huguenots. The confiscation of Church properties by Henry VIII created a powerful class for whom the reversion to Catholicism meant putting their new property into jeopardy. Such examples can be multiplied. For the 16th or 17th century political actor, the world had become more complicated. But for the contemporary political actor the increase in complexity is even greater and information on matters of critical importance is hard to come by. For example, most agree that factions, if not interest groups, play an important role in the determination of current Soviet foreign policy. Yet Adam Ulam, who shares this belief, can tell us very little about it in his excellent general history of Soviet foreign policy. Michael Tatu's excellent monograph, largely devoted to the question of the influence of factions on Soviet foreign policy during the Khrushchev period, however much it adds to our knowledge, also reveals how imperfect that understanding is. One wonders what Marxist analysts make of the fact that the *Wall Street Journal* has been opposed with mounting intensity to the Vietnam War for almost three years and with so little effect.

The larger number of actors, domestic and foreign, is not the only factor multiplying the available information. Improvements in technology and the resources available for information collection and analysis play their part. Now thousands of clerks collect information from the world press or from informants. This information is committed to paper, microfilmed, and put into retrieval systems. In the present age, unlike the earlier period, the functions of the information collector and evaluator have been separated. The contemporary information-collecting Stakhanovite is unlikely to keep writing that nothing significant has occurred since neither he nor most of his superiors knows what is significant. Masses of information and misinformation are collected. The analyst spends much of his time sifting, and the really important items are often lost in the mass of trivia. By contrast, the ambassador of the Spanish king to the court of James I was on intimate terms with the latter, had a keen idea of what was relevant to his royal master, and had to select data carefully if only because he had to write his dispatches by hand. Modern intelligence collection, by comparison, is mindless. Masses of information are collected, much of it secret, which automatically reduces the number of outsiders who can volunteer to help sort the material. To separate the wheat from the chaff is almost impossible and the memoirs of intelligence operations in World War II are replete with instances of the most significant intelligence being ignored or dismissed. The collector who is also the analyst selects the relevant and rejects the irrelevant automatically.

In view of the foregoing it seems superfluous to raise the question of further distortion of perception because of ideological predilections. Again, our ancestors seem to have suffered less than we. True, the English often saw Papists under the bed and grossly exaggerated the dangers of Spanish subversive activity. In Spain the Inquisition, whose main purpose was originally to consolidate royal authority, became an instrument which stigmatized many genuine and fervent Jewish converts to Christianity as secret Judaizers and thus inflicted a heavy blow on the Spanish polity. But the older dynastic considerations and the newer considerations of *raison d'état* did not permit ideology a monopoly in the shaping of perception. A few examples will serve to illustrate the extent of the distortion of perception by ideology in the most recent period. It was generally believed that the North Korean attack on South Korea was only a feint prior to a Soviet attack on Western Europe. Some who were anxious to build up the NATO forces in Europe seized upon the Korean War as a demonstration of the correctness of their fears and as an argument for the effectuation of their recommendations. But the belief in the danger of Soviet attack was nonetheless genuine. The major distortant was surely ideological. Anyone familiar with Stalin's history and style knew he would not have wanted two wars at once. The fear of Soviet attack in Europe derived from fears for the political stability of Western Europe and a doctrinaire belief that the U.S.S.R. would push whenever opportunity offered.

The Soviets for their part long believed in the inevitability of an economic crisis in the imperialist system and of a new series of world wars. Only the examination of the destructive effects of nuclear weapons brought Soviet leaders to review the question and to realize that their opponents also had no stomach for nuclear war.

Misperception of interest. To discuss misperception of interest in foreign affairs is to assume the existence of an interest commonly accepted as valid. Most historians deplore the religious wars of the 16th and 17th centuries and tend to define rational state interests as the aggrandizement of the power of the state without disproportionate expenditure of resources and lives. This standard is not universally valid. Those who scorn the judges and executioners of heretics and Papists, those who believe that "better dead than red" is the slogan of the ideologically bemused, and those national Communists who think that international

Communism is an abomination, nevertheless usually accept some values that transcend the cold arithmetic of national interest. Few are willing to equate all political systems and to deplore zeal wherever it might appear. In the pages that follow, the distortions that ideology introduced into the pursuit of interest will be examined without assuming that the pursuit of the national interest is automatically "right" and that ideological goals are usually "wrong."

In the 16th century the belief in the incompatibility of the two religious systems was almost complete. In the words of Garrett Mattingly: "By the 1550's neither Rome nor Geneva could envisage any end of their struggle short of the other's complete extermination. Compromise and toleration, when they were not anathema, were accepted merely to gain a breathing space and the chance for a fresh hold."[6]

This belief changed the perception of national interest. In the second half of the 16th century, for example, an irreversible deterioration of relations between England and Spain occurred despite the fact that each had a strong monarch who desired peace. Neither country could afford the expense of war. For the British, France was a great danger because Mary, Queen of Scots, a presumptive heir to the British throne, was half French, and France might well have helped her cause. Strategically, a Spanish defeat meant French control of the southern Netherlands and its ports; this was conceived to be a threat to England. For Spain the end of the English alliance meant putting the sea route to the Netherlands at risk and depending on the uncertainty of the logistic supply through Alpine passes and the Rhine. But religion and its extreme adherents, in the opinion of an excellent historian, did rally mass opinion and influence foreign policy. The Puritans in England and the Catholic exiles in Rome contributed to the decisions of the English and Spanish monarchs to go to war when it was in neither's "interest."[7]

Yet in the 17th century Cardinal Richelieu could support the Protestants in the Thirty Years War because he thereby acquired for France Alsace and the strategic forts on the eastern border which had been in the possession of the Hapsburgs. The very frequency of war offered ample opportunities for the achievement of national goals, and these opportunities often overcame religious motivations. One of the unique features of post-World War II Europe is the absence of war. The strategic mutual deterrence between the U.S.S.R. and the U.S. deriving from the fear that the

---

[6] *The New Cambridge Modern History* (New York: Cambridge University Press, 1971) Vol. III, pp. 156-157.

[7] *Ibid.,* p. 158.

employment of nuclear weapons by these powers against each other would result in the destruction of both, has extended to the avoidance of conflicts in Europe which might lead to such an exchange. In the 25 years since World War II, no shots have been fired in Europe by Communists against non-Communists or vice-versa. The only violence in Europe has been employed by Communists against heretics. If Bulgaria could recover Macedonia, if Hungary could recover Transylvania, if East Germany could recover Silesia or Konigsberg in the course of a general European war, could one predict that they would always choose the communist side? The question is quite rhetorical today, but by contrast such opportunities were frequent in the 16th and 17th centuries.

VI. *From "Struggle to the Death" to "Live and Let Live"*

In the most intense period of ideological conflicts only one orthodoxy is permitted. In the 16th and early 17th centuries Huguenots in France, Utraquists and Lutherans in Bohemia, and Protestants in Styria and the Tyrol were only tolerated until the Papacy or the Holy Roman Emperor could make the necessary political alliances to dispose of them. The Peace of Augsburg of 1555, whereby each German prince could determine the religion of his subjects, was viewed as a truce at the time. Almost a century was to pass before men recognized that the terms of the truce were essentially to be those of a settlement. Since World War II only the Communists have insisted on complete internal orthodoxy; they are more preoccupied with heresy since it challenges their justification for being. This need for validation of the system by maintenance of the validity of the ideology also inhibits the conversion of an ideological truce into a settlement.

Communists today resemble the Catholic camp during the Counter Reformation, whereas at first the U.S.S.R. seemed the analogue of the Protestant assault on the old orthodoxy. Heresy is the main problem of the multinational communist system. An obvious but perhaps useful analogy is Papal and Soviet policy in convoking the various sessions of the Council of Trent and international communist meetings. The purposes are the same: to present a common front to the enemy and to fight heresy within one's own camp. At first the Papacy hesitated to call the Council of Trent because reformists within Catholic countries would have exploited it to rehearse the well-known deficiencies of the Renaissance church. Only after a purge of dissidents was the Council convoked. By then any chances to bridge the differences had been lost, and the Council had become an instrument for the enunciation of orthodoxy. The international communist meetings have also served as a forum for attack on Soviet policies. The U.S.S.R., unlike the Papacy, has not been able to "purify" the communist parties loyal to itself, especially the non-ruling parties, and despite the exclusion of the Chinese and pro-Chinese parties, each international meeting publicly reveals wider differences. But the need for legitimization is so acute that disastrous meetings continue to be convoked.

The official custodians of orthodoxy within a system have a vested interest in continuing the internal and external struggle. The Jesuits and especially the Capuchins at first hoped to reform the church by preaching (a leaf from the Protestant book). To become effective preachers they resumed the poverty and self-denial of the old monastic orders and acquired advanced theological knowledge so as to fight the Protestants on their own ground. But in time the single-mindedness, training, and devotion which made them effective agents of re-evangelization caused their enlistment in the service of (Catholic) monarchs who were in desperate need of competent administrative staff. From preachers to the relapsed faithful, they became servants of the kings, the Capuchins serving the Bourbons and the Jesuits, the Hapsburgs. Less is known of the role of the ideologues within the socialist parties, but presumably they play a similar role.

The status quo always finds its defenders, and groups without particularly strong religious or ideological convictions become firm adherents of the continuation of the struggle when they receive material benefits at the hands of an ideologically defined leadership. Coincidentally, this phenomenon occurred twice in Bohemia and Moravia. Clerical office holders upon adopting Protestantism continued to enjoy the revenues from the lands which had supported the office. The power of appointment to such offices was often used by a secular ruler to reward supporters and scant attention was paid to their clerical qualifications. In the ambiguous situation following the Hussite heresy, such appointments were often made to Czech nobles who espoused deviant but not yet heretical doctrines. As the Counter Reformation gained momentum, these Czechs were designated as heretics and their offices transferred to German nobles presumably loyal to Vienna. As long as a grey area was permitted, peace of a kind could be maintained. But the imposition of orthodoxy caused the Protestant-leaning Czech nobility to defend itself in actions which were the immediate cause of the outbreak of the Thirty Years War, a religious struggle fought to the exhaustion of most of the parties.

In 1944 much the same issue reappeared in the Czech lands of Czechoslovakia. The defeat of the Czechs at the beginning of the 17th century had resulted in the imposition of rule from Vienna which was conducted through the instrumentality of German-speaking nobility and German-ized Czech nobility. Most of these Germans, now called Sudetens, had sympathized with Hitler before the dismemberment of Czechoslovakia and had fought for him during World War II. The Communists exploited this ancient conflict and took a leading role in the expulsion of the German-speaking populations from western Czechoslovakia. The minister responsible for the assignment of confiscated German properties to worthy Czechs was a Communist. The beneficiaries of the expulsion of the Germans, if not already Communists, became supporters of the communist coup in 1948 and of the communist regime thereafter.

As in the 16th and 17th centuries, the expellees and refugees formed a pressure group for the continuation or the revival of the struggle because only thus could they regain their property. But 20th century controls are more efficient and there is no modern analogue to the critical role played by returned Calvinist refugees in Holland and Zealand, and refugees to the north from Ghent and Brabant. Moreover, stable lines of demarcation were quickly drawn after World War II, whereas in Bohemia and the Netherlands several generations passed before lines were drawn.

The possession of land to which others have a claim is not the only economic factor furthering polarization in religious-ideological conflicts. Although much of the writing devoted to the U.S. military-industrial complex is rhetoric based on sketchy research, a vested interest does exist. The weapons-producing corporations feel no embarrassment in pointing to the ineluctable nature of the ideological conflict and the danger of letting the other side get ahead as an argument for the assignment of contracts. While little evidence of bribery has been produced, Congressmen and Senators are clearly sensitive to the loss of a contract and the dismissal of thousands of employees in their own district. General Eisenhower in his remarks about the influence of the military-industrial complex was referring to the successful effort of parts of the aircraft industry and parts of the Air Force in getting Congress to fund the production of the B-70 aircraft which he and his closest advisers thought inferior to other weapons systems. To say that the munitions makers are responsible for the cold war is to oversimplify, but that does not relieve them of the onus (or deprive them of the credit) of having a vested interest in the continuation of ideological tension.

No precisely similar institution dedicated to the continuation of the cold war exists in the socialist states because there are no private corporations to apply pressure to the Ministry of Defense. But the Soviet military leaders have been successful in beating back the most radical proposals for reduction of military forces, and there is much evidence to show that they and the "metal-eaters," as Khrushchev called the managers of heavy industry, often make common political cause.

The intelligence services also have a vested interest in the continuation of ideological struggle. The prospect that a truce might be expanded into a genuine "live and let live" agreement is unsettling to intelligence services if only because their role will be reduced. (Their belief that a truce is only an enemy ruse is usually "sincere.") The Soviet Ministry of State Security (MGB) according to scanty but persuasive evidence has sought to impede agreements. In 1964, when Khrushchev was trying to improve relations with West Germany, the MGB arranged to injure a member of the German Embassy and create an incident. The purpose was to embarrass the development of West German-Soviet understanding which Khrushchev was pursuing at the time.[8] Similarly Professor Frederick Barghoorn of Yale University was arrested in what seemed to be an effort to embarrass Khrushchev's attempt to improve relations with the U.S. In 1967 Soviet military leaders seemed to have urged the Syrians to confront Israel while civilian leaders counselled restraint.[9]

In the U.S., the Federal Bureau of Investigation is officially charged with counterespionage and has publicly opposed measures of rapprochement that would complicate the task. Mr. J. Edgar Hoover was able to overrule the Department of State, which wanted to establish Soviet consulates outside Washington, D. C. in return for permission to establish American consulates in cities outside Moscow. Many other interests and bureaucratic organizations within each state feel compelled to emphasize the dangers of accommodation. Sometimes their motivation is largely parochial, bureaucratic or material; at other times it is genuinely ideological or religious; most often the motives are mixed.

The longest and most destructive war of the earlier conflict was the Thirty Years War. Thus far in this era of conflict the Vietnam War has earned that distinction. In both cases the chief protagonists conduct the war with or through the agency of clients, some of quite minor authority. Although these minor clients could not have compelled major powers to enter a struggle, they can effectively veto its conclusion on compromise terms. Thus, for instance, Ky and Thieu in South Vietnam naturally oppose a resolution of the war on terms that would deprive them of office,

---

[8] Michael Tatu, *Power in the Kremlin from Khrushchev to Kosygin* (New York: Viking Press, 1969), p. 390.

[9] Walter Laqueur, *The Road to War* (London: Weidenfeld and Nicholson, 1968), p. 183, note.

and because of the commitment of two American Presidents to victory, they exercise a veto out of all proportion to their power. The U.S.S.R. seems to have been more eager than Hanoi, and certainly more eager than Peking, to pursue opportunities for negotiation, but since Soviet support of North Vietnam has been made a touchstone of Soviet commitment to Communism, that support cannot be withdrawn because the North Vietnamese do not follow the Soviet prescription for negotiating with the Americans. The investment of American prestige in the Vietnamese conflict is better understood.

The policy of the Nixon Administration combines exasperation with the problems of war inherited from Democratic predecessors, continued belief that one communist victory will cause dominoes to topple, and fear of alienating the right wing of the American polity. President Nixon, in particular, suffered his own greatest political defeat in the California gubernatorial election in 1962—largely because of the hostility of the right wing of the Republican Party of California to his comparatively moderate policies. The Nixon Administration would like to see the war in Vietnam terminated for domestic political reasons, but only if it can be presented as a victory over Communism or at the minimum as a contest where the Communists have not been victorious.

The Soviet interest in the continuation of the war is more related to the role of the U.S.S.R. in the world communist movement than to vetoes from internal groups. Khrushchev pursued a policy of abstention in Vietnam, but his successors were forced to more vigorous action by the U.S. bombing of North Vietnam. Failure to support a civil war in South Vietnam and failure to aid a socialist country under direct attack by the U.S. presented very different challenges to the Soviet claim to leadership of the socialist world.

The actors, institutions, and constituencies inclined to postpone or veto steps in order to end the Vietnamese conflict are largely organized. An effective impulse to change from "struggle to the death" to "indefinite toleration" or coexistence requires the belief that no side can win, and that the acceptance of a stand-off sooner rather than later is cheaper. But such a general retirement of ideological pretensions cannot settle an ongoing, hotly fought battle. Internal forces within each camp must gather enough strength to force a mutually acceptable solution on opposing groups within their own camps who see victory in sight or are unwilling to accept the costs of compromise or defeat—even though they cannot present a convincing winning strategy.

During the Thirty Years War the chief sufferers from the war were the weak and divided German states over whose territories the war was waged.

The logistics of that time made it necessary for the mercenary armies to live off the land and in a prolonged war this meant confiscation of seed grain and destruction of working livestock, i.e., famine. The Germans for whom the Thirty Years War was a total war did not have the power to end it. While the fortunes of war seesawed and the Swedes hoped that they might extend their territory to the southern shores of the Baltic and to Protestantize all of Germany, they persisted. The French withdrew their subsidies to the Swedes when too complete a Swedish victory threatened to convert the Swedes from French clients to rivals. The Thirty Years War was concluded, not because the victims were exhausted, but because each of the Great Powers was either exhausted, had achieved its aims, or had decided that its most ambitious aims were unattainable and too costly.

The analogy with the Vietnam War is obvious. The nature of the technology available to the U.S. and the problems of operating in an alien culture have caused tactics to be employed that are as destructive or more destructive of the lives of the population than that of the mercenaries of the Thirty Years War. But the sufferings of the Vietnamese do not constitute the strongest pressure for the conclusion of the war. The war can only be concluded when pressure groups stronger than the groups with a vested interest in the continuation of the war are developed. Since the U.S. is so big and Vietnam so small, it takes years of frustration and escalation to affect the American political system to the point where those who want to break off are more powerful than those who want to continue.

One striking difference exists between the conclusion of the Thirty Years War and the probable conclusion of the Vietnamese struggle which may be the Peace of Westphalia of the 20th century. The Counter Reformation had succeeded in rolling back the Protestants in Styria, in the Tyrol, in Bohemia, Poland, and the southern part of the Netherlands. The outlines of the settlement were almost arrived at years before the Treaty of Westphalia concluded the Thirty Years War, but minor participants and groups within the major states were able to exercise a veto. The Papacy and the ideologues could point to some reconquests. Although the peace did not represent the high watermark of the Counter Reformation, it was not the low watermark either. By contrast it now seems that a conclusion of the Vietnam War sometime in the 1970's will be on less favorable terms than could have been reached in 1961 or 1964. Then the neutrality of Laos and Cambodia was probable and the neutrality of South Vietnam possible and Thailand probably would have remained a Western ally. Such a solution would have restored the pre-imperialist balance of power in Southeast Asia. But now it seems more likely that a coalition government in South Vietnam would be a prelude to a communist-controlled Vietnam including Cambodia and Laos, with Thailand neutral. The necessities of internal politics make it difficult for a vastly superior power like the U.S. to accept defeat. Yet it is difficult to discern a method of imposing defeat on the North Vietnamese. Although the Counter Reformation fought against disunited Protestant opponents, it was itself divided by the contest between Hapsburg and Bourbon, i.e., between France on the one hand and Austria and Spain on the other. At the present writing the end of the Vietnamese struggle is not in sight and the manner in which it will be concluded will greatly influence U.S. domestic and foreign politics, and the role of ideology in U.S. foreign policy. These great uncertainties make predictions about the future of alliance systems in the next section tentative.

VII.   *The Future Structure of Alliances*

The distinguishing feature of the present system of alliances is the formal stability of its parts, a circumstance that owes more to the influence of nuclear weapons than to ideological consistency. In the 16th and 17th centuries nationalism often worked at cross purposes with the ideological imperatives of Catholicism and Protestantism. In the 20th century nuclear weapons tend to inhibit the free expression of the forces which ideological conflict by itself might have set in motion. Whereas nationalism in the 16th and 17th centuries reinforced the existing tendency of states to align and realign, nuclear weapons have had the opposite effect. In the 16th and 17th centuries only geographical distance or great disparity of power made war between two nations most improbable or very brief. But shortly after World War II, war became almost excluded as a possibility in U.S.-U.S.S.R. relations. Since it is quite unlikely that the U.S.S.R. and the U.S. will destroy their nuclear weapons while other states retain them, and it is even less likely that the U.S., the U.S.S.R., China, France, and whatever other powers may acquire nuclear weapons will jointly agree on their abolition, the deterrent effect of nuclear weapons on the international system may persist. This changes the system qualitatively because the two greatest nuclear powers and perhaps others in the future will be in an "adversary" relationship. The employment of this term is a novelty in the discussion of international relations and reflects the novelty of an intense rivalry between two states in which the use of the most perfected weapons is virtually excluded. This has tended to eliminate all direct hostilities thus far between the U.S.S.R. and the U.S.

This phenomenon tends, in turn, to stabilize the relationship of the secondary and hegemonial powers in alliance systems. In traditional alliances, including those of the 16th and 17th centuries, alliances served the twin function of promising territorial gains to the members of the victorious coalition in war, and of deterring the outbreak of a war in which defeat threatened the loss of territory. This situation no longer obtains in Europe. Despite the strains produced by the unresolved question of Germany and the prospects of Soviet control in Eastern Europe unravelling through the establishment of heretical or schismatic communist governments, the expectation is that the two great powers and their allies will avoid coming to blows in Europe. The traditional gains from switching alliances are no longer in the offing and penalties for departure from an alliance have been imposed by the U.S.S.R. after the fact in Hungary and prophylactically in Czechoslovakia. In Europe the U.S. has not found it necessary to contemplate the imposition of discipline on France when it reduced its participation in NATO, because there was no French advantage in joining the Warsaw Pact. It might be argued that the U.S. was prepared to intervene in Italy in 1948 if its Communist Party had come to power, and that this constituted a form of compulsion since the threat influenced the policy of the Italian Communist Party. But such pressure is of marginal significance. Western European countries do not consider joining the Warsaw Pact because it offers no gains.

Since there is either little to gain or much to lose in leaving one or the other alliance systems, the constellations are stable by comparison with the past. But to posit rigidity would be anti-historical and contrary to presently observable tendencies. Four tendencies toward change can be isolated.

The tendency toward less cohesiveness. The secondary and the tertiary members of each alliance system can establish or restore relations with members of the opposite system whom the hegemon has put beyond the pale. Thus, Peru, Bolivia, Chile, and Venezuela are now scouting the restoration of diplomatic and economic relations with Cuba. If this movement develops further, the nature of the Organization of American States (OAS) would be altered since the U.S. dominance would be successfully challenged.

In Europe, Rumania has established diplomatic relations with West Germany against the wishes of the U.S.S.R. The invasion of Czechoslovakia has prevented further indiscipline and at present the U.S.S.R. regulates the negotiations of Warsaw Pact members with West Germany. But when the German question is resolved, and it seems to be a case of "when" rather than "if," Warsaw Pact states will probably have more freedom of action.

Departure from an alliance without realignment. The Sino-Soviet alliance is virtually terminated, but neither has joined the rival system. It is theoretically possible for the U.S.S.R. or China to ally itself with Japan or the U.S. or both. But both the importance of ideology for internal legitimacy in the U.S.S.R., and to a lesser extent in the U.S., and the absence of a powerful third enemy against whom the two major powers could ally, make it unlikely that departure from an alliance will eventuate in realignment.

Neutralization or nonalignment of some members. Yugoslavia was the first state to leave one of the alliance systems and to adopt neutrality. More such cases are possible. If the Communists are victorious in Vietnam, Thailand may revert to neutrality, and if U.S. economic aid to Latin American countries declines, some may move to a neutral position. It is also theoretically possible that some NATO powers, after a legal settlement of the German question, may opt for neutrality, but it seems more likely that they will reduce their participation after the French example or deny their allies the right to station nuclear weapons on their territory (like Norway and Denmark). Legal neutralization is unlikely because it promises no benefits and may entail some economic costs.

The passing of polarization in the Third World. The penalities and rewards for nations in the Third World to align themselves with one camp or another are much reduced. The Cuban experience has introduced a new understanding into the relations between the U.S. and the U.S.S.R. The U.S. seems to have learned (the Dominican case being classed as the last act of prophylactic intervention), that small countries in Latin America can become socialist countries without radically altering the international balance of forces. With this realization the rationale for intervening before it is too late is weakened and a "wait and see" attitude tends to prevail. Therefore, reforming or modernizing regimes, which start the process with the popular expedient of confiscating or expropriating American properties with minimal compensation, feel less necessity for joining the other camp as the only means of protection against a likely U.S. intervention. The recent "low profile" of the U.S. in the face of Peruvian expropriation of private property is an example of what may become greater U.S. flexibility. This tendency is reinforced by the reluctance of either of the superpowers to assume formal obligations as a replacement for a client relationship. In the area of the most active rivalry between the U.S.S.R. and the U.S., namely the Near East, neither the U.S.S.R. nor the

U.S. is eager to exchange its client relationship with Egypt in the one case and Israel in the other for a formal alliance. If this is true in an area where war has occurred recently and where peace is not in sight, it is much more true for other areas.

In the developing areas, traditional alliance politics have much more scope for action. An alliance for a war to gain territory has a rationale and several such wars have occurred in the areas not allied to either of the systems. Besides, in poor and struggling societies nationalism is a better basis for legitimacy than socialist or non-socialist economic development. It is easier to wage a "just" national war than to make significant economic progress.

The future of alliance systems might be diagrammatically presented as consisting of a center of two fixed points, the adversary but not enemy relationship of the U.S. and the U.S.S.R. to which China may be added. Beyond this inner circle the second rank powers, particularly in Europe, assert increasing independence but do not depart from the alliance. Outside of Europe some aligned powers may become neutral and become virtual or actual members of the outer ring. In the third and outer ring the nonaligned countries are mobile among themselves but not disposed to adhere to the alliances of the central powers.

EUGENE B. SKOLNIKOFF

The International Functional
Implications of Future Technology

Technological advance and the increasing application of technology have had profound effects on the international issues confronting nations, effects often quite different from those originally anticipated on common sense grounds. Technology, instead of minimizing consciousness of national sovereignty, *seems* to have exaggerated it; instead of discouraging the emergence of weak, small states, has made proliferation of states possible; instead of bringing about sharp changes in the attitudes and assumptions of governments toward foreign affairs, has allowed continuation of "traditional" approaches to the workings of the international system.

This essay will outline some of the future international implications of continued rapid developments in technology, with emphasis on the impact of technology on international intergovernmental machinery. Likely technological developments, in a time frame of 10-20 years, are going to generate important performance demands on the international system going well beyond, in scale and intensity, the requirements placed on the

Eugene B. Skolnikoff is Professor of Political Science and Chairman of the Political Science Department at MIT. He has long been interested in the interaction of technology and foreign affairs, both from policy and scholarly perspectives. From 1958 to 1963 he was in the White House on the staff of the President's Special Assistant for Science and Technology. He is the author of *Science, Technology, and American Foreign Policy* (MIT Press, 1967) and many articles in related fields. He is also chairman of the Science and Public Policy Studies Group, a national organization of universities working in the field.

Prepared for delivery at the Sixty-sixth Annual Meeting of the American Political Science Association, Biltmore Hotel, Los Angeles, California, September 8-12, 1970.

system today. These demands will result from the increasing constraints on independent national action coupled with much more intensive requirements for international activities carried out by international machinery. Moreover, because of the diffusion of decision-making with regard to many technologies, these demands have a certain "inevitability" which means they cannot be prevented or ignored by governments. The conclusions drawn will raise important questions about the viability of the prevailing model of the international system: sovereign states vying for security and advantage, with the primary locus of decision-making within the states. They will also raise questions about the ability of the existing international machinery and the existing attitudes of governments to cope with the changed situation. The actual technical situation justifies a position somewhere between the apocalyptic and the complacent. There are in a variety of areas, particularly pollution, the seeds of unparalleled disaster. More information could show that the world now faces irreversible environmental changes that require drastic and urgent international political action, though available information does not support such a conclusion.[1]

The specific functions of international organizations can be represented in the following typology:

A. *Service*
   1. Information exchange
   2. Data-gathering, analysis, and monitoring of physical phenomena
   3. Consultation and advice
   4. Facilitation of national and international programs
   5. Coordination of programs
   6. Joint planning
   7. Small-scale funding

B. *Norm Creation and Allocation*
   1. Data-gathering and analysis for establishment of norms
   2. Establishment of standards and regulations
   3. Allocation of costs and benefits

C. *Rule Observance and Settlement of Disputes*
   1. Monitoring adherence to standards and regulations
   2. Enforcement of standards and regulations
   3. Mediation, conciliation, and arbitration
   4. Appeal of standards and regulations
   5. Adjudication

D. *Operation*
   1. Resource and technology operation and exploitation

[1] *Man's Impact on the Global Environment,* Report of The Study of Critical Environmental Problems (SCEP) (Cambridge, Mass.: M.I.T. Press, 1970).

2. Technical assistance
3. Conduct of research, analysis, and development
4. Financing of projects

I. *Environmental Alteration*

This is perhaps the newest major technological subject to receive critical public and political attention. Suddenly, governments find themselves under growing pressure to protect the "environment." Every international organization is also directly involved in some way; for a few, it is becoming a significant part of their activities. Developments of technology for deliberate manipulation of the weather, already extant or likely, can be thought of conveniently in three categories: micro-modification, modification of storms, and large-scale climatic modification. The inadvertent modification of weather or climate is also possible.

The evidence associated with cloud-seeding experiments in micro-modification suggests that rainfall can be increased locally from 5 to 20%. T. F. Malone anticipates that by 1980 "naturally occurring rainfall can be either augmented or diminished locally by proven techniques" and that by the end of the 1980's "the probability is high that rainfall several hundred miles downwind from the site of the operations can be increased or decreased at will."[2] Problems are sure to arise within countries and between nearby countries with regard to water distribution. Second, a need for international cooperation in operational matters is likely also to emerge, for at times the actual seeding may have to be done over foreign territory or international waters. Eventually, a different kind of international issue will emerge: how to allocate what is, in effect, the finite resource of atmosphere-borne fresh water. Clearly, a major problem of international resource allocation will exist.

The prospect of being able to divert or suppress hurricanes is now with us. Experiments in the U.S. (August 1969) using silver iodide appear to have been successful in reducing the maximum velocity of Hurricane Debbie by 31 and 15% on alternate days.[3] If modification activities could deflect the course of a hurricane, the possibility of claims for damage or water deprivation could result. Operational activities with regard to hur-

[2] T. F. Malone, "Current Developments in the Atmospheric Sciences and Some of Their Implications for Foreign Policy," in *The Potential Impact of Science and Technology on Future U.S. Foreign Policy,* Papers presented at a Joint Meeting of the Policy Planning Council, Department of State, and a Special Panel of the Committee on Science and Public Policy, National Academy of Sciences, June 16-17, 1968, at Washington, D. C., pp. 82-97.

[3] "Advances in the Eye of a Storm," *New Scientist,* December 25, 1969, Vol. 44, No. 681, p. 630.

ricane modification must necessarily be carried out in an international environment, even at times over several different national territories. Also on the technological horizon are bold schemes for melting the Arctic ice cap by means of chemicals (carbon black), a dam across the Bering Straits (often proposed by Russian scientists), dispersing the Arctic cloud cover, or pumping warm Atlantic water into the Arctic basin.[4] The purpose would be to alter radically the climate of the Northern Hemisphere, in particular to warm and provide increased moisture for the vast Siberian region. The probable effects of removing the Arctic ice cover vary from forecasts of entirely benign and beneficial effects (more temperate climate with increased rainfall in Siberia, Europe, and as far south as the Sahara), to predictions of the onset of a new ice age and substantial increases in the ocean level as the Greenland ice cap melts. Obviously much more information of the likely effects is required before any such project can be allowed to proceed. But, it must be realized that the resources required for such a project may *not* be beyond the capabilities of a single large state (a Bering Straits dam is entirely feasible at costs comparable to large continental dams). Moreover, if the economic payoff is as fantastic as warming Siberia, the incentive to proceed would be enormous. What international machinery does the world have to govern such a project?

Weather modification technology can also lead to strategic or tactical military capabilities, thereby affecting the balance of power. It can be used as a weapon in economic warfare, diverting water needed for agriculture or hydroelectric power. Conversely, it can be used as a tool for enhancing economic development and welfare. Such uses of this technology may depend critically on the international means developed for controlling it, for allocating its benefits, and preventing its misuse.

This technology depends directly on increased scientific understanding of the atmosphere. The underlying research and data-gathering is being carried out partially under national auspices, but the major components are two international programs associated with the World Meteorological Organization (WMO) and the International Council of Scientific Unions (ICSU). One is called GARP—the Global Atmospheric Research Program—and the other the World Weather Watch (WWW).[5] These two related programs may themselves create important requirements for new or revised international machinery to operate the programs when they are farther along. The potential implications of the knowledge gained through

---

[4] P. M. Borisov, "Can We Control the Arctic Climate," *Bulletin of the Atomic Scientists,* March 1969, Vol. XXV, No. 3, pp. 43-48.

[5] Malone, *op. cit.,* p. 87.

the international programs also establish a requirement for, in some sense, "controlling" the application of the knowledge in accordance with internationally agreed purposes.

Inadvertent modification of weather and climate is occurring as a natural concomitant of this century's accelerating application of technology, the growth of the world's population, and the urbanization being experienced in all countries. The world *could* be heading for a major catastrophe. From 1880 to 1940, the average temperature of the earth increased by 0.4°C, while in the last 25 years, the temperature has decreased by 0.2°C.[6] Are these climatic fluctuations of the last 80 years natural variations, or a result of man's activities? There are a number of ways in which man's activities could disturb the atmospheric heat balance.

One is the accretion of carbon dioxide in the atmosphere, as would be expected from an increased consumption of fossil fuel. The result of a CO_2 "blanket" is to trap solar energy reflected from the earth's surface, creating a hothouse effect. The accretion of CO_2 would correlate with the increase in the earth's temperature until 1940, but not with the subsequent decrease. A possible explanation of this phenomenon is that the CO_2 concentration is being overwhelmed by atmospheric particle pollution. That is, dust from urban, industrial, or agricultural activities can affect the thermal balance primarily in the opposite direction to the CO_2. The dust forms a barrier to solar radiation, thus reducing the energy reaching the earth. In addition, the dust forms nuclei for low-level cloud formation which serve to reflect some additional solar radiation back to space. "At present, on the average, about 31% of the earth's surface is covered by low cloud; increasing this to 36% would drop the temperature about 4° C, a drop close to that required for a return to an ice age."[7]

There are also other possibilities of considerable concern. The earth's albedo (the percentage of incoming solar radiation directly reflected outward) is being changed by man-made alteration of the earth's surface. Dense urban areas and highways reflect more radiation than forest or agricultural land. These changes could also lower the surface temperature. Additionally, there are unknown factors such as rocket exhausts in the upper atmosphere which may affect the transfer of radiation, or water vapor exhaust from jets and SST's which spread ice crystals at very high

[6] Gordon J. F. MacDonald, "The Modification of Planet Earth by Man," *Technology Review,* October-November 1969, Vol. 72, No. 1, pp. 27-35. The information that follows is drawn from this article, except where noted.

[7] Reid A. Bryson and Wayne M. Wendland, "Climatic Effects of Atmospheric Pollution," presented at the American Association for the Advancement of Science National Meeting, December 27, 1968 (mimeo) quote some of this evidence.

altitudes producing a haze and cloud cover with undetermined, but potentially significant, consequences.[8] The list of possible calamities could be considerably extended. But the simple point is that there is a good probability that the changes in the atmosphere brought about by "multiplying man's" multiplying use of technology are leading the planet to significant climatic changes. This danger may arise in critical form within the next twenty years.

The world has already seen several dramatic illustrations of premeditated large-scale actions with potentially substantial global environmental effects. The fallout from atmospheric atomic tests is one example. Others have included high-altitude U.S. and Soviet nuclear tests and the orbiting by the U.S. of a belt of copper filaments for a military communications experiment. The latter two illustrate the interesting kinds of problems these capabilities raise.[9]

In the case of both the U.S. 1962 high-altitude nuclear shots—called Project Starfish—and the copper filament experiment—Project Westford —, advance notice of the experiments was given by the U.S. Government. In both cases, extensive analysis was made within the U.S. of the predicted long- and short-term effects of the experiments. In the Westford case, in fact, the government made impressive efforts to publicize the analysis in advance, and to encourage scientists in other countries to make their own analyses. This did not prevent a substantial negative reaction from the world scientific community. The Westford experiment followed the predictions exactly: the filaments have fallen out of orbit as expected.[10] The same cannot be said for Project Starfish. Rather, there were substantial effects that did *not* accord with the predictions: some of the released electrons became trapped in the earth's magnetic field, with some long-lasting effects on scientific experimentation.[11]

Two points must be noted in these examples. One is that the scientific analysis prior to the experiments was not infallible. The other is that the U.S. Government, even though it demonstrated substantial responsibility in allowing prior publication and analysis of security-related experiments, was still prepared to proceed unilaterally in the face of doubts raised by

[8] Bryson and Wendland, *ibid.*

[9] See Eugene B. Skolnikoff, *Science, Technology and American Foreign Policy* (Cambridge: The M.I.T. Press, 1967), pp. 84-92, for an extended discussion of the communications experiment.

[10] I. I. Shapiro, "Last of the Westford Dipoles," *Science,* December 16, 1966, Vol. 154, No. 3755, pp. 1445-1448.

[11] Bernard Lovell, "The Pollution of Space," *Bulletin of the Atomic Scientists,* December 1968, Vol. XXIV, No. 10, pp. 42-45.

the worldwide scientific community, and in the face of the knowledge that miscalculations would affect the entire globe, not just the U.S.

Several lessons for the future requirements for international machinery emerge from this listing of only a few phenomena associated with man's large-scale tampering with the environment. It is essential that we know more about the processes of the environment to plan for the full range of effects that will follow specific large-scale actions. Machinery to control technology could take many forms, varying from independent national capabilities to some kind of "impartial" international body. Machinery with a genuine international capability would necessitate development of ancillary mechanisms for appeal, adjudication, monitoring, enforcement, and assessment of damages and claims.

It may be necessary to contemplate international responsibility for, or even international operation of, some large-scale technology as a way of guaranteeing equitable distribution of benefits and genuine concern for possible harmful side-effects. The high cost of some projects may also force them into the international arena.

With a rapidly growing population and with rapid increases in industrialization and urbanization, both the needs and the wastes of society grow at exponential rates. A world population expected to grow to nearly 5.0 billion by 1985 from a little over 3.5 billion in 1970 would lead to more than a 40% increase in requirements for food, energy, and natural resources just to maintain the present unsatisfactory economic levels.[12] These requirements will, in fact, be substantially increased by the economic growth levels in all countries and the corresponding increase in industrialization. But to meet these requirements it will be necessary to use massive quantities of fertilizer and insecticide, transport and burn growing quantities of fuel, dispose of more agricultural and industrial waste, transform more agricultural land into houses and highways, cut down more forests, find more fresh water supplies, etc. All this will substantially alter our present environment and add substantially to the environmental pollution problem. It is not a single problem, but an enormously complicated interrelationship. The implications of a change in one aspect cannot be approached adequately without consideration of the total system.

The use of DDT and related organochlorine compounds to control insect pests has been a major factor in making it possible to feed and im-

---

[12] United Nations Economic and Social Council, "World Population Situation," Note by the Secretary-General, doc. E/CN.9/231, September 23, 1969 (Population Commission, 15th Session, November 3-14, 1969).

prove the health of the present world population. But now we realize that the accumulation of these persistent pesticides in the food chain is toxic to some forms of animal life. Many animal species have been endangered, and the background concentration for man has in some cases exceeded presently accepted limits. Perhaps the most disturbing recent development is a report that DDT interferes with photosynthesis of marine phytoplankton, a phenomenon that could have catastrophic effects on the living resources of the sea.[13] Several countries have now banned, or severely curtailed, the use of DDT-related compounds; the U.S. acted in mid-October, 1969. There is controversy as to whether effective substitutes for DDT are available. When they are, the costs are likely to rise. Thus, we quickly come to hard choices between starvation or disease on one hand, and gradual accretion of DDT levels on the other, between economic growth and stagnation. Who is to make these choices? Are there alternatives? Ultimately, who pays? It is instructive that in present debates in the U.N. and other international bodies, the developing countries are understandably much less concerned with pollution problems than the developed countries.

The industrial sulphur effluents of one country are claimed to come down as sulphuric acid in another.[14] The problem can be solved most easily by using sulphur-free fuels, but that would cut off the market for oil from the Middle East and Venezuela. Oil pollution at sea, with attendant serious effects on bird and marine life and on recreation, becomes a grave menace as the size of tankers increases in order to satisfy growing energy-demands of civilization. A single accident can become a disaster; and the exploitation of seabed oil resources, with the likelihood of occasional accidents, is sure to increase sharply in the near future. Whatever measures are taken to reduce these risks, they will, at the least, raise the price of oil—with political consequences.

The general problem of solid waste disposal has astonishing dimensions. In the U.S. alone, the magnitude of solid wastes today is estimated to be 140 million tons of smoke and noxious fumes, 7 million automobiles, 20 million tons of paper, 48,000 million cans, 26,000 million bottles and jars, 3,000 million tons of waste rock and mill tailings, and 50 trillion gallons of hot water along with a variety of other waste products.[15] The

[13] Paul R. and Anne H. Ehrlich, "The Food-From-The-Sea Myth," *Saturday Review,* April 4, 1970, pp. 53-65.

[14] Kenneth Mellanby, "Can Britain Afford to be Clean?," *New Scientist,* September 25, 1969, Vol. 43, No. 668, pp. 648-650.

[15] United Nations Economic and Social Council, 47th Session, "Problems of the Human Environment," Report of the Secretary-General, doc. E/4667, May 26, 1969, p. 5.

waste problem is aggravated by the conscious development of plastic and other containers that are not degradable in the environment.

The expected growth in the use of nuclear power as a major source of energy will greatly aggravate the problem of safe disposal of atomic waste, which in turn may change the economics of the nuclear power industry. Even the relatively low-level release of radioactivity from "normally" operating nuclear power plants may be a severe problem.[16]

Implications of Environmental Alteration for International Functions. Research, analysis, and information about the changing environment are needed rather desperately. The goals are several:

a) simply to know on a continuing basis what, in fact, is going on;
b) to determine the likely effects of present trends, and to establish tolerances;
c) to develop alternatives to, or modification of, current practices when necessary; and
d) to establish hard data on the costs and benefits of alternative courses of action for political decision.

This is clearly the most immediate set of requirements, and one that has been recognized now by many international organizations.[17] Developing the information is the (politically) easy part of the job. The implications of the information for further action will prove more difficult.

The primary need is for establishing international norms for effluents, for solid waste disposal, for tanker routing, for actions in the event of ship accidents, etc. Free flow of trade, in fact, will also require uniform standards among nations. Where pollution has more subtle effects, and requires for its amelioration unaccustomed domestic limitations in certain fields, the political problems will be more serious. For example, if limitations are required on the amount of grassland covered over each year (as regarding the earth's albedo), or if limitations must be put on the total use made of specific technologies each year, then we will be seriously affecting areas never before subject to any form of international regulation (or in many countries even national regulation). Limitations on research and development itself may even become a serious political issue if a judgment can be made that the direction new technology may take

[16] Barry Commoner, "Attitudes Toward the Environment: A Nearly Fatal Illusion," address for presentation at Unanticipated Environmental Hazards Resulting from Technological Intrusions Symposium, Annual Meeting of the AAAS, Dallas, Texas, December 28, 1968, (mimeo.).

[17] "Problems of the Human Environment," Report of the Secretary-General, *op. cit.,* which lays out the general objectives of the U.N. Conference on the Human Environment to be held in Sweden in 1972.

would seriously exacerbate environmental problems. The prospective technologies of peaceful use of nuclear explosions and weather modification, and the actual technologies of supersonic aircraft might be limited.

Creation of norms implies other functions as well, especially the question of allocation. The costs of setting standards, or of banning the use of certain technologies, will not be evenly distributed. The costs of giving up or replacing some pesticides and herbicides will not only be measured in dollar terms, but also in terms of human life and health. Similarly, the costs of controlling industrial waste will fall unequally on certain nations because of their particular geographical positions, their dependence on certain resources, or their emphasis on certain industrial processes. Who should pay—the producer, the consumer, or the nations most offended by the particular pollutant? How is this to be determined? Moreover, a nation's competitive position in international trade may be substantially affected by the measures it must take. Regulations must, therefore, be international simply to maintain fair competition; universally-applied regulations may damage the competitive position of some countries, thereby raising issues of equity.

The allocation function requires an appeals and adjudicative mechanism. A means of developing technical analyses which are recognized as fair and impartial will be essential. A damage assessment and claim procedure will be necessary to settle violation of the international standards. Finally, a monitoring and enforcement procedure is implied to insure compliance. This could continue to be "passive," as is generally the case now, in the sense that nations tend to conform voluntarily to standards on the basis of a calculation of their own best interests. A more "active" means of enforcement may be necessary if the present pattern is not adequate.

II. *The Oceans*

The oceans have been the focus of some of man's earliest technological developments, and also his first attempts at codifying international law. Today, they are the scene of application of the latest technology, and as a result the cause of much re-thinking and re-shaping of international law. Rapidly advancing technology for underwater extraction of organic and mineral resources; improving knowledge of the likely extent of the resources, especially seabed oil; and continued exponential growth in energy demand—all combine to make the political and legal questions associated with ocean resources controversial. Technological developments, spurred by the promise of high return on investment, will make it possible to operate in deeper and deeper underwater environments. With the expectation that the "world's greatest supplies of fossil fuels" lie on the continental rise, one can quickly see both the motivation and potential payoff of technological developments.[18] Other resources of the seabottom are also of potential interest, particularly manganese, nickel, copper, sulphur, and the "detrital" minerals.

The major international questions, of course, have to do with who owns the resources on or under the seabed; thus, who has rights beyond the continental shelf to their exploitation and to their benefits? Whatever institutional arrangement is established for regulation of the seabed, it would not only have to have a means for deciding who has access to the seabed, but also a procedure for distributing publicly whatever benefits accrue. In addition, a means for monitoring and enforcing decisions, regulations, and standards could well become necessary, whether it was carried out by an international mechanism, or by agreement among national entities.

There are several important aspects to the international issues surrounding living resources of the sea. One is the trend in present fishing practices and technology related to maximizing yields. It is a controversial issue, but some scientists estimate the potential harvest of the sea to be not very much greater than present annual harvests (about 60 million metric tons). The Food and Agriculture Organization (FAO) estimates less than twice the present catch size as the likely maximum that can be expected.[19] In fact, with improved technology and greater fishing effort, *depletion* of fish resources would result unless effective control methods are undertaken. A second aspect is the increasing knowledge of the migratory patterns of fish. This knowledge can create difficulties if it allows a nation to take fish that have been traditionally harvested by other nations at a different stage of the migratory cycle, or if the fish are taken at a stage of the cycle before they breed. A third aspect is the possibility of aquaculture, that is, artificially improving the nutritive value of the sea, and "raising" fish.

There are several other oceanic activities of great economic or political importance which will also be the focus of extensive technological development in the near future. Transportation will go in the direction of larger and faster vessels and probably true submersibles. Military applications will tend toward larger and quieter nuclear missile submarines for the deterrent force, more devices for submarine detection, and probably

---

[18] P. M. Fye, A. E. Maxwell, K. O. Emery and B. O. Ketchum, "Ocean Science and Marine Resources," in Edmund A. Gullion, ed., *Uses of the Seas*, The American Assembly, Columbia University, (Englewood Cliffs, N.J.: Prentice-Hall, 1968), pp. 17-68.

[19] Food and Agriculture Organization, Committee on Fisheries, Fifth Session, Rome, April 9-15, 1970, "Fishery Aspects of the Indicative World Plan and Proposed Follow-up," doc. COFI/70/3, January 26, 1970.

also more anti-submarine forces. With the increasing vulnerability of land weapons, the undersea missile launchers will steadily take on more importance, possibly replacing land-launched missiles entirely. The undersea environment will inevitably be a primary focus for arms control measures, as it already has.

In view of these increased uses, the problem of congestion of the ocean environment arises. Many applications are pertinent to the same areas of the ocean, potentially congregating ships for fishing and transport, submarines, unmanned buoys, and permanent drilling platforms in the same vicinity. Entirely new regulations and rules of the road may have to be developed.

Implications for International Functions. Whatever regime is established for the deep seabed, it will have to be concerned with the exploitation of resources beyond the limits of national jurisdiction. Presumably, licensing authority would be involved, which means establishing criteria and making choices. If that regime is given genuine management responsibility for the seabed, or ownership of the resources, then the whole ramification of functions from licensing through norm creation, rule observance, appeal, adjudication, and operation all follow.

For fisheries regulation, one sees the same basic functions: denying benefits and rights to one country in favor of another; the existence of machinery for appeal, monitoring, and enforcement of decisions; and an ability to develop or obtain independent technical information. Similar steps will be necessary to prevent the serious depletion of protein-supplying species endangered by overfishing. With rather less impact, the need to handle the growing congestion resulting from uses of the seas will also require international machinery.

III. *Outer Space*

The space-launching powers will undoubtedly continue space activities, though with less political urgency.[20] The interest in receiving economic returns from space, and in minimizing the costs by sharing, will undoubtedly grow. Satellite applications that can assist in the planning and management of forestry and agriculture activities are almost certain develop-

---

[20] The information for this section comes from many sources, but in particular the report of the U.S. National Academy of Sciences, National Research Council, "Useful Applications of Earth-Oriented Satellites," Washington, D. C., 1969 and "Selected Space Goals and Objectives and Their Relation to National Goals," Battelle Memorial Institute Report No. EMI-NLVP-TR-69-2 to NASA, July 15, 1969.

ments during the time period of interest. Based on the ability to scan large areas with a variety of sensor devices, satellite systems will provide invaluable information for allocating water use, anticipating crop size, and many other land management activities. Such services are likely to become essential once they are adopted as a regular input to a nation's economic system.

Another exciting application of satellites is in the search for mineral and organic resources. It is quite likely that satellites can be used to prospect for minerals, or at least to identify promising locations for ground exploration. Such information may have considerable economic and strategic interest, raising troublesome questions about information control and access, control of the application of this technology, and international operation.

The number of satellites serving as relay communications systems will increase substantially in order to meet the expanding demand for communications channels. The systems themselves are likely to be increasingly sophisticated, with much larger channel capacity, well-defined beam (geographical) coverage, increased power, and other specialized capabilities. Whether there will be a single global system or multiple national systems is not clear at this time. The demand for frequencies will add enormously to the problems of allocation of the frequency spectrum. Direct broadcasting from satellites to augment home or community antennas is under development today. The U.N. Working Group on Direct Broadcast Satellites estimates that direct broadcast into community or augmented home receivers will be technically feasible by 1975.[21] However, the actual development of direct broadcast systems will depend on complex economic, political, and technical criteria.

The increased interest in observing the planet and its environment for research, exploration, exploitation, monitoring, and enforcement purposes will lead to the development of satellite-centered data-gathering and dissemination systems. These will be sophisticated satellites, with their own sensors, and tied to sensors and read-out stations throughout the globe. Such systems will also add to the pressure for frequency and orbital space allocations, and will raise questions of international versus national management, economic efficiency, security of information, joint planning, etc.

Expansion in air transportation, as well as introduction of high-speed marine transport, will require greatly improved navigation aids, a need

[21] United Nations, Committee on the Peaceful Uses of Outer Space, Report of the Working Group on Direct Broadcast Satellites, doc. A/AC.105/51, February 26, 1969.

very much in evidence today in transatlantic air routes. Satellite navigation systems are likely to offer the most attractive answer to such needs. Adequate allocations for frequency and orbital requirements, as well as the question of management, will again be central.

Functional Implications of Space. These stand out quite clearly, and, in fact, have already resulted in the creation of several new international institutions, most notably INTELSAT, the consortium for communications satellites, and the European cooperative space research and launcher development organizations (ESRO and ELDO). The first functional international requirement will be operating mechanisms for many of the systems mentioned above. In most cases, national ownership and operation will not be adequate as a permanent arrangement for political reasons. Some of the information generated by the space capabilities will have serious economic and even strategic consequences, most notably information on likely new resources, on fish movements, and on weather. Important questions about the ownership of the information and its availability to national or commercial interests will have to be dealt with by international means.

Whole fields of human activity will come to depend on some of the systems once they are in operation—for example, weather forecasting, navigation and air-traffic control, and crop-planning. For reasons of equity and political feasibility, therefore, there will be strong pressure that these be internationally-run systems. Many of the systems may involve differential application costs as well as differential benefits to some portions of the globe. Questions of allocation of benefits and costs, and of pricing policy will, therefore, have to be dealt with by international machinery. Some communication systems may have a profit potential, or at least seriously affect the profit potential of existing land-based systems in the same fields. Complex problems of equity will have to be settled through international action. The procurement of equipment will also raise questions of economic equity. Which countries will receive development and procurement contracts? INTELSAT is plagued with this problem now. The desire to share in the economic and technological benefits of development and production of communications satellites is clearly one of the motivations behind competing proposals.

Interest in spreading the costs of space development and exploration is likely to encourage more cooperative space efforts than are envisioned today, possibly involving international machinery in the process. Direct broadcast satellites will raise thorny problems of technical standards for the satellites themselves, television standards, regulation of broadcast coverage and interference (including jamming), and, of course, frequency and orbit allocation. Some form of international control of broadcast content cannot be excluded. Greatly increased activity in the near-earth environment will, in turn, require a space regime capable of establishing norms and making allocations for various contemplated uses. The existing and potential military uses of space (essentially surveillance, communications, and tracking) will greatly complicate that task.

IV. *Natural Resources*

The availability of natural resources—mineral, organic, and hydrological—is a perennial source of concern. Whatever the short-term situation, the world has a finite supply of mineral and fossil fuel resources. The world's demand for metals has been growing at a rate of more than 6% per annum for nearly a decade.[22] The entire metal production of the globe before World War II was about equal to what has been consumed since. Some materials are, or soon will be, in short supply: helium, mercury, tin, silver, manganese, chromium, titanium, tantalum, and tungsten.[23] Of these, helium and mercury have unique properties and no satisfactory substitutes are presently known. The nuclear-energy minerals have the same character. Thus, mineral conservation measures may be required and would have to be of international scope to be meaningful. The present situation seems to be that not as much is known as should be about the actual global resource situation.

The assumption that the market mechanism can be relied on to call forth new supplies from lower-grade ores is not valid for those metals in which sharp discontinuities of concentration occur. Lead, zinc, and mercury show this characteristic, as do some of the more common metals outside of their basic ore deposits.[24] The assumption that cheaper energy can make extremely low-grade ores profitable ignores the fact that low-grade ores would require enormous costs in the handling and processing of rock.[25] A persistent and vexing problem is the efficient use of existing resources in the light of future needs rather than of present technology and economics.

Functional Implications of Resource Scarcity. The most immediate neces-

---

[22] T. S. Lovering, "Mineral Resources from the Emerged Lands," in *Potential Impact, op. cit.*, p. 43.

[23] Preston E. Cloud, Jr., "Approach to Assessment of the World's Mineral Resources," in *Potential Impact, op. cit.*, p. 30.

[24] Lovering, *op. cit.*, p. 39.

[25] *Ibid.*

sity is international development of a geochemical census of the earth's crust in order to determine the real resource situation. The uneven distribution of the world's resources, and the uncertain extent of those resources, may together create increasing pressure for an international approach to their management and efficient use. The U.S. and other developed countries are, by far, the largest consumers of raw materials today, and may be preempting the possibility of other countries using those resources for their own future development. This could become a serious political issue producing pressures for machinery to manage, allocate, and regulate the use of resources. In addition, the growing use of resources has a direct relationship to the pollution problem. Regulations growing out of the need for pollution control may well be realized as limitations on national consumption of various kinds of raw materials.

V. *Food*

The Green Revolution of the late 1960's, which appears at least to have postponed a threatened worldwide famine, is a coincidental product of several factors: timely development of new technology in the form of new seed strains, good weather in critical areas, and the willingness of farmers to plant the new varieties. But this development is only a temporary reprieve, not a long-term solution, as long as population pressures continue to increase. The FAO's "Indicative World Plan for Agricultural Development" (IWP) designed to highlight food-related issues and requirements until 1985, points out that agricultural production on the average must show an annual average increase of between 3.2 and 3.8% as compared to the average 1962 figure of 2.8%, a substantial long-term change in the average.[26] Moreover, this assumes no change in already inadequate levels of food quality and caloric intake. If some increased demand is also postulated, the annual increase required for developing countries will be 3.9%.[27] In short, the danger of a catastrophic worldwide famine is likely to be with us for a long time.

Functional Implications of Food Problems. The international implications largely depend on one's point of view, a different situation from some of the other topics discussed here. It is conceivable that the situation will remain roughly as it is: concern and limited attempts to help, some international machinery devoted wholly to the problem, but in the main a

---

[26] G. Cheld, "Famine or Sanity," *New Scientist,* October 23, 1969, Vol. 44, No. 672, pp. 178-181.
[27] *Ibid.*

national approach. It is also possible that the food and larger development problems will receive increasing attention from the world community as a whole, and lead to substantially new or expanded functions on the international scene including management and allocation of resources—money, fertilizer, pesticides, water, machinery, etc.—to bring about adequate food production, distribution, and quality. The particular kind of event that could bring about such functional developments most rapidly would be the onset of a major crisis, whether it be widespread famine or some environmental crisis.

VI. *Population*

Population control is without question the single most serious environmental problem the world will have to face in the next 50 years. From the economic, the cultural, and the sociological points of view, it appears essential that population growth be brought under control. But that clear imperative encompasses many problems. One is simply: how? Others involve judgments about optimum sizes of populations, distributions among races and nations, motivations, and other issues of considerable subtlety and sensitivity. It is clear that the finite resources of the earth, including open space, cannot support a continuously expanding population indefinitely. And whatever the optimum size of population may be, the preservation of at least some present Western values would be jeopardized by populations very much larger than those postulated by 1985 or 2000 (in excess of 6 billion). Of course, values may change along with population growth and new technology, as they have today in comparison with the past.

A time may come when enforced birth control is unavoidable. This social control may well be based on international, at least as much as national, considerations. In the immediate future, direct intervention in birth control will probably remain an individual, or at most a national, matter. But the international consequences of unchecked birth rates are likely to create substantial political pressure for restrictions which will have to be universally applied, or at least universally agreed upon. This, in turn, implies some kind of international negotiation and international machinery to help carry out the agreement. There remains the question of how birth rates can be controlled even if there is the personal or political will to do so. Many legal, sociological, technical, and psychological birth control techniques are now in use, most centered around the idea of family planning. The family planning approach is sound, but the decision is left in the hands of the family itself. It is entirely possible that individual preferences may keep the birth rate up too high on the average, even in developed, long-lived societies.

At the same time, the prospects are not good for development of chemical agents that might be adequate to the task, due to legal and political problems at least as much as to technical ones. One definition of adequacy implies a chemical that has long-term effects so that only one dose is required. The most desirable goal would seem to be an agent that produces indefinite sterility, but is reversible on a temporary basis. If state control is ever required, such a technology would be the easiest to adapt. However, present practices for developing and testing new drugs make it most unlikely that any such drug could be developed.[28] The difficulties are that: 1) new drugs are tested by the FDA in the American environment, not the environment of other countries; 2) safety requirements are so stringent that development of new drugs are discouraged on cost grounds, and the prolonged test period impedes influencing the population problem soon enough; and 3) there exists no independent national or international scientific body of appeal to which FDA decisions can be presented and challenged on scientific grounds.[29] To the extent that the necessary technology for population control is yet to be developed—a controversial point since many believe that existing technology used in the family planning approach, coupled with health and development programs will do the job— some new international procedures will be required to change the ground rules for that development.

VII. *General Observations*

Stanley Hoffmann has observed succinctly that "The vessel of sovereignty is leaking." The consciousness of independence and license for nations to do as they please, mentioned originally, is illusory. Many technological developments today make it a partial truth at best. Self-interest in the use of many technologies makes it mandatory for nations to reach agreements that constrain their freedom of action, for to do otherwise would deny the use of the technology, or bring about various forms of retaliation. The constraints are usually freely entered into, and in that sense can be thought of as self-imposed, but they are nevertheless limitations on sovereignty. What is striking is how far this erosion of sovereignty has already gone. Essentially all of the functions which will be necessary by the 1980's in fact have their counterparts today. Some are

[28] Carl Djerassi, "Prognosis for the Development of New Chemical Birth Control Agents," *Science,* Vol. 166, No. 3904, Oct. 24, 1969, pp. 468-473.
[29] *Ibid.*

rudimentary and *de facto*. But others, even in the politically difficult regulatory area, are surprisingly extensive and effective. The status of today's functionalism is critical in evaluation of the capability of the existing international system to evolve into what will be required in the 1980's. However, even if the entire complex of intergovernmental organizations were performing well today, the increase in the tasks and responsibilities of the system that will be called for in a very few years will not be realized unless conscious steps are taken now to prepare for that time. Moreover, the general performance of international machinery today, notwithstanding its effectiveness in some areas, leads to considerable skepticism that it provides an adequate base for expansion and increase in responsibility without substantial modification.

The growing constraints on freedom of national action, and the increased responsibility flowing to international organizations, will mean that the locus of decision-making will increasingly be forced from the national to the international arena. Nations will not necessarily lose their voice in the control of specific issues, but an increasing number of issues will have to be settled in an international environment. It seems quite likely that there will be a tendency for interest groups within nations to look increasingly to the international organizations in their area of concern, accentuating the expansion of international decision-making.

A countervailing trend, however, will be the growth in political and economic saliency of the technological subjects discussed here. Of relatively marginal interest to governments in the past, their implications will force them closer to the center of the political stage. Inevitably, that will also imply greater national sensitivity to any loss of control, and thus increased resistance to any delegation of responsibility to international bodies over which governments exercise only limited control. That could also mean that these subjects will begin to look more like the "high politics" issues of national security and power relationships of today, and become more central concerns of governments.

But these issues are so pervasive in society, and cut across so many of the direct concerns of individuals and interest groups, that governments will never be able to speak with a single voice in these matters. In fact, the problem of integration of policy at the national level, often raised with regard to the effective operation of international organizations, will become even more difficult. It may be that we must look to the international level to provide the necessary integration, rather than primarily to the national level. If so, it is another example of the way in which the focus of decision-making is likely to move toward the international scene.

The nature of the issues emerging from advancing technology and its side-effects emphasizes the connectedness of things. Increasingly, issues can not be neatly divided into boxes labelled "oceans," "agriculture," "health," and so forth; rather, they interact with each other. This is no less true domestically than internationally and will be a major problem in the future, making current questions of jurisdiction and coordination of international organizations pale into simplicity. Additionally, the complexity and size of modern technological and organizational systems make the task of innovation exceedingly difficult.

We can point to what may be the hopeful beginning of increased public interest in some countries in the substantive issues that have been raised in this analysis, particularly environmental control and pollution. It will surely take such public interest, expressed in political activity, to bring about the kind of controls on man and his works, whether national or international, that will be required for survival. Accompanying this increased public interest in protection of man's environment there seems to be a growing recognition that governments do not have the right to act unilaterally in technological areas when the effects may spread beyond national borders. It remains to be seen how this recognition will develop, but it will be a prerequisite for substantial movement in the direction of international decision-making.

There is also, at least in the U.S., a disturbing reaction to technology itself, a reaction which could take on dangerous "Luddite" aspects. To the extent that the solutions to technology-caused problems may lie in technology itself, this anti-technology reaction could seriously inhibit progress toward protecting the future. It may manifest itself first in pressure to keep budgets for science and technology to a minimum and to exercise tight control in those very areas that are essential for understanding and ameliorating the physical and social problems the world faces.

The political environment in which international organizations will have to function will also change. Developments in the nuclear arms race and political tension in general will substantially affect the possibility of meeting the issues raised here. Political developments between the superpowers will obviously have a profound influence on the evolution of international machinery. China must be a part of the resolution of these technology-related issues. One can anticipate major conflicts of interest becoming serious sources of tension between North and South.

Whatever the political developments of the next two decades, "inevitable" technological developments will pose major new demands on the international system. Determination of the optimum course of system evolution must depend, in part, on an evaluation of existing international machinery in terms of requirements for the next 20 years. Whether "evolution" will be enough, or whether we will need a "revolution" in the existing international order, is a controversial judgment. Will governments and organizations recognize the extent of the problem in time, even if moderate change in the system would be adequate? Clearly the need for understanding the issues involved is urgent.

WILLIAM D. COPLIN

International Organizations in the Future International Bargaining Process: A Theoretical Projection

By focusing on the international bargaining process,[1] this essay seeks to project the role of international organizations in the international politics of the next 20 years.[2] It is assumed that in the future the international political system will continue to be characterized by its current decentralized structure, and that the state will remain the primary international bargaining agent. The manner in which international organizations affect the ways states bargain with each other must therefore be examined.

William D. Coplin is Associate Professor of Political Science and Director of the International Relations Program, Syracuse University. He is the author of *The Functions of International Law* and *Introduction to International Politics: A Theoretical Overview,* and the editor of *Simulation in the Study of Politics.*

[1] For a discussion of the utility of the bargaining framework in the study of international law and related institutions see William D. Coplin, "Current Studies of the Functions of International Law: Assessments and Suggestions," in James A. Robinson, ed., *Political Science Annual II* (New York: Bobbs-Merrill, 1970), pp. 149-208. For an introductory presentation of bargaining concepts as an approach to international politics see William D. Coplin, *Introduction to International Politics* (Chicago: Markham, 1971), pp. 257-291.

[2] A discussion of recent approaches to the future can be found in Herman Kahn and Anthony J. Wiener, *The Year 2000: A Framework for Speculation on the Next Thirty-Three Years* (New York: Macmillan, 1967) and Daniel Bell, ed., *Toward the Year 2000: Work in Progress* (Boston: Beacon Press, 1969). For a balanced and systematic approach to forecasting the future of Western Europe see Donald J. Puchala, "The International Political Future of Europe," in William D. Coplin and Charles W. Kegley, Jr., eds., *A Multi-Method Introduction to International Politics: Observation, Explanation and Prescription* (Chicago: Markham, 1971), pp. 381-410.

The Future International Bargaining Process

I. *The Evolving International Bargaining Process*

There is a basic distinction between what might be called the politics of collective problem-solving and the politics of conflict:

> The difference . . . lies in the attitudes of the parties toward each other. In the former situations, the states agree that a mutual problem confronts them although they may offer different solutions and competing interests; in the latter, the states see each other's behavior as the basic problem.[3]

The important factor is the degree to which external conditions shape the bargaining relationship among states. In the collective problem-solving relationship, the environment in which the two states are operating can represent such a threat or provide such an opportunity that the two actors may find it necessary to cooperate. The environment may be important for states engaged in a conflict bargaining relationship, but it may not be so sufficiently important that the states are willing to form a coalition to deal with it. In conflict bargaining relationships, the international environment is a relatively passive factor; in collective, problem-solving bargaining, the environment becomes an obstacle against which the states form cooperative strategies.

The collective problem-solving relationship is not entirely free of competition since states continually attempt to shape costs and benefits to maximize their own interests. Similarly, conflict relationships include cooperative actions by the antagonists. Although the politics of collective problem-solving and the politics of conflict have always characterized international relations, the trend over the past 100 years is that collective bargaining among states is increasing and becoming more salient to the political interests of states while conflict bargaining is becoming less pervasive.

The international environment has been so radically transformed in the last 100 years that interactions among states have greatly changed and increased, creating a set of common problems for all states. States today are forming coalitions against the international environment to solve these problems. In short, the international environment has stimulated the opportunity, if not the necessity, for extensive collective problem-solving among states.

Certain traditional conflict issues have diminished in importance, particularly territorial and symbolic interests. The former were the most frequent sources of conflict, involving border disputes as well as control over colonial empires. During the early stages of the state system, symbolic

---

[3] Coplin, *Introduction, op.cit.,* p. 222.

issues were usually produced by religious differences or dynastic questions; more recently by differences in social ideology. Sometimes territorial and symbolic issues converged to intensify the hostilities of major antagonists (e.g., the Napoleonic Wars), while at other times they served to cross-pressure the conflict (e.g., Wars of Religion). Today, however, both territorial and symbolic issues—although continuing to provoke conflict—play a less important role in overall bargaining patterns among states.

Part of the reason for their decline can be explained by the increase in mutual problems. Extreme ideological conflict is less probable in an age where common membership in international organizations, such as the World Health Organization (W.H.O.), may be dictated by physical necessity. As states draw closer together economically, socially, and ecologically, the high-conflict relationships generated by territorial and ideological factors are not likely to be as crucial as they once were.

The other set of factors limiting the intensity but not necessarily the frequency of territorial and ideological conflict is rooted in the revolution in military technology since 1945. Fear of nuclear war has countered the desires of many leaders to engage in military adventures purely for the sake of territorial gain. Symbolically, the balance of terror exerts a continuous brake on the inclination of states to act unilaterally. Almost as important as the fear of nuclear war has been the increasing cost of occupying and dominating foreign territory. Today, states cannot cheaply engage in territorial conquest even against relatively weak powers, primarily because indigenous forces can resist for protracted periods with a relatively low probability of total defeat. The fact that almost every available piece of territory is controlled by a state capable of providing some form of military resistance further contributes to the high costs of attempting territorial conquest.

While territorial and ideological interests, as traditional sources of conflict bargaining, have diminished in intensity in response to the new high costs of conflict, the contemporary international environment may generate new sources of conflict as intense as the territorial and symbolic issues of the past. Interests surrounding the control of outer space, the high seas, and even weather modification are likely to become more intense in the next 20 years. Many of these new developments in the technological-ecological aspect of the international environment may ultimately become life and death matters for particular states.[4]

---

[4] For a general discussion of the impact of technology on conflict and cooperation in future international affairs see Eugene B. Skolnikoff, *The International Imperatives of Technology* (Geneva: Centre Européen de la Dotation Carnegie, 1970).

Whether these new issues will lead to collective solutions or to conflicts depends on many factors. The most conspicuous are the initial negotiations and general communications among the states concerned with a specific issue. Perhaps most crucial in the long run is the impact of political and bureaucratic processes within each state on the bargaining interactions among states.

Contemporary political systems in open as well as closed societies contain a large number of quasi-independent "policy-influencers."[5] Representing special interests, bureaucratic pressures, partisan politics, and mass attitudes, these policy-influencers place significant constraints on foreign policy decision-makers not only by threatening to withhold political support, but also by providing subtle cues regarding foreign policy objectives and interpretations of international events. As a result, an important indicator in the foreign policy-making process is whether or not domestic political opinion across a broad spectrum has become sensitized and mobilized on a particular international issue. When the political interests of powerful policy-influencers within a state are involved, the likelihood that any given issue will generate a conflict relationship increases tremendously. Whether or not he approves, the foreign policy decision-maker may be forced into conflict bargaining with other states over a particular interest. If the issue becomes sufficiently charged, an individual political actor may become locked into a highly personalized conflict situation, since a clear reversal of position may result in the loss of office. When this happens, he is likely to treat the bargaining relationship as if the other state's gain is his state's loss regardless of the inherent attributes of the issue itself.

The growing complexity of the international environment and of the foreign policy interests of states has stimulated the need for increasingly specialized, technically competent bureaucratic structures. This need for specialization has engendered the tendency to isolate those new interests from the arena of national politics. The complexity of this environment has allowed foreign policy decision-makers to protect many issues from partisan politics in open political systems and from the struggles of high-level political elites within closed political systems. Although technical complexity may insulate the specialized foreign policy decision-maker from political control, it may also serve to protect potentially collective problem-solving relationships from the impact of domestic politics.

Various factors determine whether or not a particular issue stimulates

---

[5] For a discussion of domestic politics employing the concept of policy-influencer see Coplin, *Introduction, op.cit.,* pp. 69-78.

broad-based reaction among policy-influencers. The nature of the interaction between the states involved may be important. Even more significant may be the interest attached to a particular issue by political forces within a society. For example, international economic questions evoke more extensive political activity in the United Kingdom than in the U.S. Ultimately, the factors determining the degree to which certain types of policy-influencers will become concerned with a particular bargaining relationship depend upon the basic political and economic conditions within the state.

Based on the previous analysis, the following projections for the nature and distribution of bargaining relationships can be made:

1. The number of collective problem-solving relationships stimulated by the new technological and ecological conditions in the international environment will greatly increase over the next 20 years, if insulated from domestic politics.
2. Conflict bargaining relationships generated by territorial and ideological interests will decrease in number and will probably continue to decrease in intensity.
3. Conflict bargaining relationships stimulated by new international conditions may increase if highly technical foreign policy issues are increasingly affected by domestic politics.

II. *The Impact of International Organizations on the Evolving International Bargaining Process*

The roles which international organizations play in the international bargaining process can be classified into three categories. The first and least demanding is the environmental role: the organization serves primarily as a forum where the representatives of states can meet to communicate and implement their bargaining strategies. Like the classical function of the neutral mediator, the environmental role of organizations is passive but often crucial in keeping lines of communication available. A second and more active role for international organizations is the regulative role. This category includes those institutional activities designed to constrain the bargaining behavior of states. Cease-fire orders of the Security Council, for example, constitute an attempt to prohibit certain types of bargaining behavior among antagonists. The regulative role may be performed overtly as, for example, peacekeeping operations by the U.N., or covertly, as a set of norms inhibiting certain types of actions. The third and most highly developed role of international organizations is to make decisions that are designed to distribute costs and benefits among states. This distributive role can be performed in various ways: a merit decision by the International Court of Justice (I.C.J.) on a legal question, or a development loan decision by the World Bank. In both cases, the institutions have taken an action that affects the distribution of some benefits to the states involved.

The following three assumptions will be employed throughout our subsequent discussion.[6] These underlie the developmental model.

1. The three roles are hierarchically interdependent so that the *effective* performance of the distributive role requires the *effective* performance of the other two, and the *effective* performance of the regulative role requires the *effective* performance of the environmental but not the distributive role.

This proposition does not posit a logical or a deterministic relationship among the three roles; nor does it imply that the distributive role cannot be performed at all unless the regulative role is already performed. Instead, it posits a relationship based on the *effective* performance of the various roles.

2. As an international organization effectively performs its more highly developed roles, the states affected by the institution will attach increasing legitimacy to the institution.

This proposition combines the concept of legitimacy[7] with the important notion of national willingness to cooperate in the operation of most international organizations. Symbols and operational effectiveness are two relatively distinct but interdependent sources of legitimacy.[8] The proposition implies that the legitimacy of international organizations must increase as they begin to perform the two higher-level roles of regulation and distribution.

3. In order for an international organization to perform effectively, member states must feel an increasingly stronger need to cooperate.

This proposition also emphasizes the importance of national commitment to the operation of international institutions. It assumes that only a set of attitudes that results in an increasing commitment to mutual cooperation can foster the solid growth of an international organization beyond the environmental role-playing stage.

The willingness to cooperate is a key variable for both the develop-

---

[6] These assumptions are unevaluated. They are accepted for purposes of discussion although they may be treated as testable propositions in another context.

[7] For example, see Seymour Martin Lipset, *Political Man* (New York: Doubleday, 1963), pp. 64-70.

[8] Although Lipset tries to distinguish between legitimacy and effectiveness, learning theory suggests that the former is generated by the latter; see Richard M. Merelman, "Learning and Legitimacy," *American Political Science Review* (1966), pp. 548-561.

ment of international organizations and for the relationships of states involved in bargaining situations. The reciprocal impacts of international organizations and collective problem-solving and conflict bargaining must be examined.

International Organizations and Collective Problem-Solving. Given the willingness of states to cooperate to solve a mutual problem, we would expect not only growth in the number and variety of international organizations,[9] but also a progressive development of their roles from environmental to regulative and finally to distributive. Surveys of the operations of contemporary international organizations[10] and comparisons with earlier eras are easily explainable in terms of such a progression. The large number of collective, problem-solving bargaining relationships that we expect to emerge in the future suggests that international organizations will continue to grow in number and to expand in impact.

A large variety of international organizations have developed recently to deal with issues involving states in collective problem-solving. Agencies like the W.H.O. represent a global response to socio-economic problems. Regional organizations like the European Economic Community and the Central American Common Market have emerged to deal collectively with economic problems. So-called regional security organizations like the Warsaw Pact, NATO, and SEATO may be viewed as examples of cooperative problem-solving in mutual military security. Finally, the general purpose organizations—the U.N., O.A.S., and O.A.U.—have, at certain times and for certain issues, developed the capacity to promote collective problem-solving among states.

We can expect that those organizations dealing with collective, problem-solving bargaining relationships (including components of general purpose organizations) will develop through the three stages in the next 20 years. In addition to increasing in number and developing beyond the environmental role, international organizations will help to generate conditions for the creation and maintenance of collective, problem-solving bargaining relationships. They may do this in a number of ways.

First, a frequent domestic consequence of coordinating a set of interests through an international organization is to envelop those interests in

---

[9] The pattern of growth of I.G.O.'s and its implications is discussed in Charles W. Kegley and J. Martin Rochester, "Assessing the Impact of Trends on the International System: The Growth of Inter-Governmental Organizations," in Coplin and Kegley, eds., *A Multi-Method Introduction, op.cit.,* pp. 401-411.

[10] For a discussion of the tasks performed by inter-governmental organizations see William D. Coplin, *The Functions of International Law* (Chicago: Rand McNally, 1966), pp. 152-163.

highly technical terms. As a result, the specialized technical format helps to shield the activities of foreign policy decision-makers from the vagaries of highly visible national politics involving a broad spectrum of policy-influencers. As noted above, the more numerous the policy-influencers interested in a particular issue, the more likely a bargaining relationship will become conflict-laden. Hence, by providing a highly specialized format in which certain types of issues are defined and approached (e.g., international economic cooperation), international organizations help to prevent conflict.

Second, the impact of international organizations may be to solidify a bargaining relationship that is not completely collective. As interests stimulated by conditions in the international environment lead to bargaining among states, the initial predisposition is usually to cooperate on an informal basis. This initial bargaining orientation could readily dissipate if a lack of responsiveness is attributed by one of the parties to the other. Once the orientations of the states begin to change, the consequence could easily be the development of a conflict bargaining relationship. Here the existence of international organizations could play a decisive role by providing an environment and structure through which communication can be more readily handled. Also, the responsiveness of the permanent apparatus of the organization relieves some of the burden of the states in responding to the cooperative overtures of other states.

Third, international organizations which play highly regulative and distributive roles act as a third force in the bargaining relationships of states. As the legitimacy of the organization increases, the organization itself will become a consideration in the bargaining strategy of each state. States will begin to consider the power and predispositions of the permanent staff of the organization. Instead of focusing its activities on one state, a state may attempt to develop a coalition among members within the organization to get action. At the very least, this concern with a new set of circumstances generated by the existence of the organization serves to place an intervening force between bargainers and therefore to decrease the likelihood of conflict.

Initial collective problem-solving involving an international organization reinforces and prolongs this bargaining relationship. Moreover, as the record of organizations becomes longer and the precedents for dealing with various kinds of issues expand, the capacity of organizations to facilitate and maintain collective, problem-solving bargaining relationships will increase.

From this analysis it would appear that issues generated by changing technological and ecological conditions in the international environment leading to collective problem-solving rather than conflict relationships can be substantially affected by international organizations. If the organizations can anticipate potential areas of collective problem-solving and establish precedents for dealing with them, they will prevent conflict. Given their capacity to provide some insulation from broad domestic political forces and to interject third party considerations, international organizations could play a large role in channeling issues into collective problem-solving structures.

International Organizations and Conflict Bargaining Relationships. Present trends and future expectations are radically different for the role of international organizations in conflict bargaining relationships. In contrast to the spectacular growth in the number and variety of international organizations dealing with collective bargaining relationships, those established to deal with conflict bargaining relationships have not become more numerous. The I.C.J. and the U.N. are the only global institutions which have a primary role in the containment of conflict bargaining relationships. At the regional level, the Organization of African Unity, the Organization of American States, and the Arab League exist in part to deal with conflict.

The reason for their smaller number and lack of sustained growth is the threat of violence in conflict situations. Although we have noted a lessening of the salience which states attach to certain conflict issues, the potential for violence still remains. This requires some centralization of conflict resolution capability by the community of states. Technical expertise is not required to deal with specific conflict issues to the extent that it is required to deal with collective problem-solving issues. The resolution of a conflict issue depends less on a positive action at a technical level (as it does for collective problem-solving issues) and more on choosing alternatives implicit in the contentions of the two states.

Organizations seeking to control conflict or to provide an environment for conflict bargaining relationships can only succeed if they are able to mobilize a substantial collective commitment from those disinterested in the distribution of the payoffs of a particular issue. Consequently, the development of a large number of organizations to deal with conflict bargaining relationships in a large variety of substantive areas or even a large combination of small regional areas would be counterproductive. It is very likely that the fewer members in a given organization, the less chance that disinterested states could be found among the membership of that organization for resolution of a dispute between two of its members. Since conflict-control capabilities are scarce and result when states pool their influence, the fixed number of institutions does not appear to represent a failure of these organizations to affect the control of conflict, and in fact it may very well be an important factor in the limited success they now enjoy. The future growth of one or two additional regional organizations similar to the O.A.U. may contribute to the overall impact of international organizations on conflict bargaining. However, any further regional fragmentation may very well result in the loss of what control now exists over conflict.

The second trend is the lack of growth in the business of the existing conflict-control organizations. Because the regional organizations have played a relatively small role until very recently, our analysis must focus on trends in global institutions, comparing the Permanent Court of International Justice (P.C.I.J.) and the League of Nations on the one hand to the I.C.J. and U.N. on the other. A comparison between the organizations of the prewar and postwar periods should help to forecast the future roles of the I.C.J. and the U.N.

In a recent study focusing on two-party conflicts involving independent states, it was found that there has been no growth in the business of the postwar organizations.[11] Table 1 indicates that the P.C.I.J. handled more cases in fewer years than the I.C.J.

TABLE 1

Number of Two-Party Conflict Cases for the P.C.I.J., League, I.C.J. and U.N.

	Number of Cases	Cases Per Year of Operation
P.C.I.J.	24	1.26
I.C.J.	23*	1.05
League	35	1.75
U.N.	31	1.41

* Adjusted for unilateral unanswered submissions employed by the U.S. and the U.K. to embarrass Warsaw Pact members.

Similarly, the average per year for the League is greater than for the U.N. The doubling of the number of nations since the Second World War has presumably increased the number of conflict relationships in the interna-

---

[11] William D. Coplin, "The P.C.I.J., I.C.J., League and U.N. in the International Bargaining Process: A Comparative Analysis With Some Implications for the Future," paper presented to the American Political Science Association Annual Convention, 1970. The empirical data for this paper is available from the Comparative International Political Studies Project of the International Relations Program, Syracuse University.

tional system, so the figures represent a striking decline in actual, relative to the potential, business of the two organizations.[12] The regional organizations, particularly the O.A.U., are picking up some of the slack.[13]

One should not conclude, however, that the environmental role of the U.N. has stagnated or declined. While the I.C.J. may be in eclipse, the overall environmental role of the U.N. is greater than it was for the League. First, the role of the U.N. in such issues as Kashmir and the Arab-Israeli dispute has consumed a great deal of its energy and perhaps has limited its capacity to deal with less volatile issues. Second, many issues not formally treated by the U.N. are discussed informally by governmental representatives in U.N. locations. Third, much like the intervention of the Federal government in labor disputes in the U.S., the U.N. exists as a real threat of outside intervention that shapes the bargaining strategies of states. In short, the lack of growth in business for the U.N. (when compared to the League) does not necessarily mean a decline in its environmental role in bargaining interactions among states. On the contrary, it may be evidence that its role has become more extensive at the covert level and more intensive at the overt level.

Such an interpretation might lead one to make the following predictions. First, relatively low-salience conflict issues will be submitted to the U.N. less frequently over the next 20 years. Second, because states will not want to incur the costs (e.g., loss of domestic political flexibility, loss of control), foreign policy decision-makers will attempt to limit their bargaining strategies sufficiently to avoid outside intervention by other states as well as the U.N. Third, the U.N. will continue to play a major role in high-salience issues by representing the interests of the majority of states in limiting the bargaining strategies of the major antagonists. Not only will one or both states involved in the conflict bargaining relationship not be willing to bear the cost of U.N. intervention and therefore seek to limit their own strategies, but once an issue threatens to involve directly a large number of states, there will be overwhelming pressure to have the U.N. intervene directly.[14]

---

[12] This conclusion is also based on the assumption that the amount of conflict in the post-World War II system was equal to the amount in the interwar period. Such an assumption may not be warranted given the comparative inactivity of Germany and Japan. However, it is not unreasonable to assume that the increase in the number of states generated a sufficiently large increase in the number of conflict bargaining relationships regardless of the level of conflict throughout the system.

[13] Carnegie Endowment for International Peace, *Synopsis of United Nations Cases in the Field of Peace and Security* (New York: 1966), pp. 66-74.

[14] This projection and the general discussion of the regulative role of the U.N. are more relevant to bargaining relationships other than those that have developed between the

A positive relationship between the salience of an issue and the probability of overt U.N. intervention in the bargaining relationship can be predicted. Since we can expect lower-salience conflict issues in the future, there may be fewer occasions for overt intervention by the U.N. in such bargaining relationships, but there will be continued U.N. activity. This prediction assumes, however, that if the bargaining relationships likely to be generated by technological and ecological developments stimulate conflict relationships, the U.N. may become extremely busy in dealing with high-salience conflict bargaining relationships in the next 20 years.

A third trend is the decline in the distributive role performed by organizations in conflict relationships. Evidence of this decline is presented in Table 2.[15] In the pre-World War II period, the higher percentage of joint submissions can be interpreted as an indication of a greater willingness on the part of the participants to allow the organizations to make distributive decisions. Further evidence can be found in the higher percentage of merit decisions by the P.C.I.J. compared to the I.C.J. and the more frequent suggestion for a final settlement (as opposed to a regulative action such as a cease-fire) by the League compared to the U.N. Unlike the organizations dealing primarily with collective problem-solving, the development of these four organizations has not proceeded in the linear fashion suggested by the developmental model.

TABLE 2

Percentage of Joint Submissions and Substantive Distributive Decisions
for the P.C.I.J., I.C.J., League, and U.N. (Percent of Total Cases)

	Joint Submissions	*Distributive Decisions*
P.C.I.J. N=24	42	67
I.C.J. N=31	9	91
League N=35	23	69
U.N. N=31	0	100

One explanation for this apparent decline of distribution is provided by the developmental model itself. The legitimacy which states attach to in-

---

U.S.S.R. and the U.S. The assumption behind both the proposition and the discussion is that the two superpowers will continue to exhibit the self-constraint evident since the Cuban Missile Crisis.

[15] This table is based on data discussed in footnote 11.

ternational organizations today is less than it was during the pre-World War II period. Located geographically and culturally in the West, most of the prewar states had strong symbolic commitments at least initially to the organizations that developed out of their common socio-cultural and historical experience.[16] The rise of Hitler and World War II helped to destroy much of this symbolic attachment and the entrance of a large number of anti-Western states did even more. As a result, the legitimacy necessary for the I.C.J. and U.N. to develop distributive roles is insufficient and accounts for the unwillingness of contemporary states to accept the distributive function of these organizations.

On the question of legitimacy alone, one might expect that the regional organizations have a better chance of developing a distributive capacity in the future. The O.A.U. is certainly not a prisoner of the Western tradition and may in the future develop the trust among its members necessary for the development of distributive functions. Although the O.A.S. suffers from an image of U.S. dominance, it is possible that the states of Central and South America may come to accept a distributive role for it. Whether or not other factors will also contribute to the growth in the distributive role for these and less well-established, general purpose organizations dealing primarily with conflict bargaining relationships, remains an open question.

Another factor that may account for the movement away from the distributive role by international organizations can be found in the changing nature of the international bargaining process. As noted earlier, territorial issues have become less salient in the contemporary period. At the same time, conflict bargaining issues seem to stimulate inflexible domestic political constraints so that foreign policy decision-makers are highly limited in the types of distributive outcomes they can accept. Together, these two developments seem to have generated conditions which force political leaders to choose the continuation of a conflict bargaining relationship instead of a final resolution of the issue through a distributive outcome. This approach to bargaining permits the continuation of conflict within certain regulative constraints.

Some evidence of this proposition can be found by comparing the behavior of the victors following the two World Wars. After World War I, the victors appeared to have most strongly valued a definitive territorial settlement. The Versailles Treaty and a series of smaller related treaties

---

[16] See the A.P.S.A. paper cited in footnote 11 for a discussion of the change in the geo-cultural characteristics of members from the P.C.I.J. and League to the I.C.J. and U.N., pp. 20-24.

made definitive distributions in territory and reparations. Although some questions were left open, there was a serious commitment to settle as much as possible. In contrast, after World War II, the victors made tentative territorial decisions that for all practical purposes have become definitive. Although this tentativeness was a result of disagreement among the victors, it appears to have set the tone for bargaining strategies and outcomes in the postwar world. Rather than reaching bargaining solutions, states today apparently feel the need to allow issues to remain unsettled even though relatively high levels of hostility may eventually result.

While the environmental role of the I.C.J. and U.N. has become less overt for most conflict relationships, the regulative role of the U.N. has increased. As noted, the tendency for states to avoid international institutions does not necessarily mean that the international institutions do not have some kind of impact on almost every conflict relationship. In fact, it may indicate that the institution has come to symbolize a set of norms, operating at an implicit level, that encourages states to regulate themselves in conflict bargaining relationships.

In those conflict situations where self-regulation has failed, the U.N. has begun to operate in a more direct regulative capacity. The development by both political leaders and scholars of "peacekeeping," as opposed to "dispute-settling," rationales for the U.N. is evidence that the U.N.'s role has become primarily regulative.[17] The U.N. appears to be most effective in its role of constraining bargaining interactions so that they do not exceed certain geographical bounds and force-levels in conflict situations. At the symbolic level, the U.N. has come to serve as a living representation of the will of those states committed to restricting the bargaining interactions of states much as potential political supporters in domestic systems demand legal rather than extra-legal strategies from political antagonists.

In predicting the future role of international organizations in conflict bargaining relationships, we must take into account the factors that have led to the decline of the distributive role. Part of this retrenchment is a natural outcome of the legitimacy crisis which the postwar international organizations have had to face as a large number of relatively non-Western states have become participants in the system. Some is a result of the changing nature of conflict issues and the willingness of states to live with conflict and, conversely, to avoid distributive decisions. Finally, part of

---

[17] For example, U Thant has written "there has tended to be a tacit transition from the concept of collective security . . . to a more realistic idea of peace-keeping in a changing world," in David A. Kay, ed., *The United Nations Political System* (New York: Wiley, 1967), p. 76. Also see Jack Citrin, "The United Nations Peacekeeping Activities: A Case Study in Organizational Task Expansion," *Denver Monograph Series in World Affairs,* Vol. III, No. 1, 1965-1966.

this retrenchment may be a consequence of the realization that the international bargaining process must be regulated before organizations will have the capability to make distributive decisions.[18]

Based on these developments, the following predictions of the role of international organizations in conflict bargaining relationships over the next 20 years can be made:

1. International organizations will play an environmental and regulative rather than a distributive role;
2. The I.C.J. will not increase its business while the U.N. will operate more covertly in all but high-salience issues;
3. Regional organizations may develop some distributive capability since they may gain legitimacy more quickly than the global organizations;
4. International organizations will increase in their capacity to maintain general constraints on the bargaining strategies of states.

III. *Conclusion: Toward the Institutionalization of the International Bargaining Process*

These predictions represent a 20 year perspective on the role of international organizations in the international bargaining process. A long-range and aggregated effect could be the institutionalization of the process. In the distant future, it is possible that most international interests of states will be pursued either by mobilizing the actions of international organizations or by conforming to their regulative norms. This will not be the dawn of a new world. It will no more generate world peace, develop an effective instrument to pursue world public policy, or avoid intensive political antagonisms than the institutionalization of domestic political bargaining. Rather, the politics of collective problem-solving and the politics of conflict will continue to be pursued, although their form and issue-content will have been altered. Whether the new form will allow man to maximize his values or lead him to pursue more honorable purposes than he has previously, will continue to depend on the men who participate in the new institutional arenas. Ultimately, the long-range institutionalization of the international bargaining process will depend on what happens in the next 20 years. Hopefully, the existing international organizations will continue to play the role they have played in recent years, first by helping states to conceive of issues in collective problem-solving terms and second by containing the potential for violence inherent in conflict relationships.

---

[18] This point ties into the emphasis on the effective performance of the three roles as the key to their hierarchical interdependence. The League may have failed because it attempted to play a distributive role in the international bargaining process before it had sufficiently developed its regulative capacities.

TILDEN J. LeMELLE AND
GEORGE W. SHEPHERD, JR.

Race in the Future of International Relations

Although Western scholarship has largely failed to recognize its importance, race has become the central problem of international politics. Disciplined analysis has lagged behind events, and little systematic attempt has been made to relate the racial factor to theories of international relations. In sum, no consistent analysis has been applied to the problems of international racial conflict and integration.[1] However, the impact of race may well revolutionize international studies as we come to understand

Tilden J. LeMelle is Associate Director of the Center on International Race Relations, Graduate School of International Studies, University of Denver. He is a Visiting Associate Professor of International Relations, specializing in black studies and African politics.

George W. Shepherd, Jr. is Director of the Center on International Race Relations, Graduate School of International Studies, University of Denver. He is a Professor of International Relations, specializing in race relations, American foreign policy, and African government.

This paper was originally prepared for delivery at the Sixty-sixth Annual Meeting of the American Political Science Association, Biltmore Hotel, Los Angeles, California, September 8-12, 1970.

[1] See George W. Shepherd, Jr., "The Study of Race in American Foreign Policy and International Relations," *Studies in Race and Nations,* Vol. 1, No. 4 (1970), Center on International Race Relations, Graduate School of International Studies, University of Denver. For a detailed analysis of U.S. "integration" as colonial-type assimilation, see Tilden J. LeMelle, "Ideology of Blackness, African-American Style," *Africa Today,* Vol. XIV, No. 6 (December, 1967), pp. 2-4. Also see Karl Deutsch, "Research Problems on Race in Intranational and International Relations," in George W. Shepherd, Jr.˙ and Tilden J. LeMelle, eds., *Race Among Nations* (Lexington, Mass.: Heath Lexington, 1970), pp. 123-152. Only a few earlier and prophetic analysts, such as W. E. B. DuBois, Richard Wright, and Gunnar Myrdal, have identified the significance of race in transnational relationships.

how racial stratification influences national behavior and sets a world pattern of conflict. This article will suggest a conceptual framework of racial stratification and examine some of the future problems of international race relations.

Racial stratification exists when the availability and distribution of individual choices in society are determined by membership in a particular racial group, and is, in effect, racial discrimination against a subordinate racial group. Thus, in a racially stratified system, class stratification is a function of racial stratification and the boundaries of the two are highly coterminous.[2] Racial stratification systems have many variations, but we are primarily concerned here with white dominance systems. In these systems dominant groups have a high color consciousness and a high technical capability with which they subordinate other groups perceived as nonwhite.[3] White dominance social systems are found in high capability Euro-American societies which perceive themselves to be dominant internationally. These societies have manifested a history of Darwinian imperialism which reached its peak in the colonization of Asia, Africa, and Latin America. The conflicts and wars of the first half of this century were in large measure the result of rivalries between white dominance powers; the revolutions of the second half are primarily the result of the colonized asserting their identity and refusing to accept a continued status of servility.[4]

I. *The Function of Race in White Dominance Systems*

All racially stratified systems tend toward dysfunction. In such systems race functions initially as the basis for establishing and regulating dominant and subordinate relationships by means of subjection and/or pseudo-assimilation.[5] In this stage race acts as a system-wide *centripetal* force drawing together all racial components under the assumed superiority of the dominant (and solely legitimate) racial group. With the breakdown of subjection and pseudo-assimilation, race functions as a divisive factor

[2] See G. W. Shepherd, Jr., "Comparative Policy in White Dominance Systems," paper for a Conference of U.N. Institute for Training and Research (UNITAR) and the Center on International Race Relations on Public Policy and Racial Discrimination, Aspen Institute, 1970.

[3] See T. Shibutani and K. Kwan, *Ethnic Stratification, a Comparative Approach* (New York: Macmillan, 1965). Richard Schermerhorn's work, a conflict analysis of dominant-subordinate group relations, is important. His modification of an earlier conflict model of group relations is found in *Comparative Ethnic Relations: A Framework for Theory and Research* (New York: Random House, 1970), pp. 22-25.

[4] A. R. Preiswerk, "Race and Colour in International Relations," *The Yearbook of World Affairs*, Vol. 24 (1970), London Institute of World Affairs, p. 58.

[5] Cf. Tilden J. LeMelle, "Black Power and the Integration/Assimilation Myth," in Lenneal J. Henderson, Jr., *Black Political Life in the U.S.* (San Francisco: Chandler, forthcoming).

leading to open inter-racial conflict. At this stage race acts as a *centrifugal* force fragmenting the system along its already racially stratified lines. Thus, in a white dominance system, race is not only the rationale for and a continuing cause of discrimination, but it is also the catalyst for eventual violence between dominant and subordinate racial groups and for societal distintegration. These general principles are applicable to the analysis of international as well as national race relations.

II. *White Dominance Centripetal Systems*

Prior to the emergence of non-white nationalism in the mid-20th century, race functioned as a regulative force for maintaining stability both in white-dominated states and in the white-dominated international system. Inter-race relations were a matter of white control over subordinate racial groups either through subjection or emanation[6] or a combination of both. Patterns of racial stratification remained relatively stable and racial discrimination (a function of the convergence of racism and power) served as an instrument for regulating mobility, power, and the distribution of values in inter-race relations.

The centripetal white dominance system is best characterized by its value assumptions which are messianic and ethnocentric. Virtue is assumed to exist primarily in what is white and Western, and evil is equated with blackness and the assumed irreligious ways of non-white societies. These values, which blend color and culture, have explicitly justified slavery, the color bars of the Southern U.S., apartheid in South Africa, and even the discriminatory laws regulating Indian lands and non-white immigration.

The organization of power in the centripetal system enthroned and perpetuated the white dominance system. Violence was used to conquer the non-white and was then legalized as police and vigilante power to protect the privileges of those who controlled the land and production as well as the government. Police force and military power were the ultimate weapons by which the stratification pattern was enforced. Affection for the law and the lawmaker was taught as a special virtue, but for those non-whites who broke the law there was little justice, *only* swift punishment.

Limited mobility within this general centripetal system was available

---

[6] The concepts of "subjection" and "emanation" are used in the same sense as that employed by Manfred Halpern in "Applying a New Theory of Human Relations to the Comparative Study of Racism," *Studies in Race and Nations,* Vol. 1, No. 1 (1969), Center on International Race Relations, GSIS, University of Denver. Emanation in this case means the acceptance of the legitimacy of white rule by subordinate groups.

only to those non-whites who rejected their own heritage and race—in short, who became assimilated.[7] Historically, the extent of mobility has varied with the depth and intensity of non-white culture, with the perceived economic threat which mobility represented to the white man, and with the level of production and job opportunities.

Thus, the centripetal pattern of white dominance held together as long as dominant and subordinate groups accepted assimilationist values, respected and feared discriminatory legal and police powers, and hoped that limited mobility could lead to a better life. At different times and places in the 20th century this centripetal race system has been broken and reversed. In some states it still continues. The historic breaking point has varied greatly. In the U.S. it was the rise of Black Power in the 1960's; in the United Kingdom, the colonial rebellion begun by Gandhi in the 1930's, fostered the black immigration and demands of the post-war period; the French fought bloody colonial wars against Asians and Arabs in the 1940's and 1950's and today confront angry Algerian workers in the streets of Paris. South Africa and Australia employed discriminatory and repressive devices which came under stringent attack from non-white indigenous populations. White dominance responses have varied from civil rights laws in the U.S. to colonial immigration barriers in the U.K. and brutal suppression in South Africa. Yet all have failed, despite temporary compromises, because the centripetal white dominance system, giving up subjection and insisting upon assimilation as the price of equality, has denied non-whites full equality.

III. *Centrifugal White Dominance Systems*

The basic new pattern in white dominance systems is a centrifugal or conflict pattern in which race no longer serves as an adequate regulatory device but rather designates lines of open conflict between white and non-white within and between nations. Increasingly race is being transformed from a suppressive or assimilationist device into a rallying point for self-determination by non-white groups which have become self-conscious and power motivated. The promise and denial of equality by white dominance systems have been the contradictory thesis and antithesis which have spurred subordinated racial groups to reassert their selfhood and cultural pride.

---

[7] Slavery, the U.S. color bar, and apartheid were aversive-suppressive and subjective rather than assimilationist. See Joel Kovel, *White Racism: A Psychohistory* (New York: Pantheon, 1970).

Conflict rather than assimilation or integration is characteristic of this phase. Within nations this means the formation of interest and political groups along racial lines, the strengthening of racial community consciousness, and the growth of counter-racist attitudes among subordinate and dominant groups. Riots and rebellion are frequently the product of the self-determination drive of non-whites, and in irreconcilable situations the ultimate conflict, racial war, arises. A state of mind which Manfred Halpern has called *incoherence*[8] develops in the white and non-white groups due to the breakdown in assimilationist, consensual goals and in communication. Riots in U.S. urban centers, uprisings of Africans and riots of colored in South Africa, clashes with police in London and Paris, Black Power demonstrations against whites in the Caribbean, and aboriginal demonstrations in Australia all dramatize the emergence of a centrifugal conflict pattern of race relations. These patterns are not uniform; different levels of violence exist; and various national and regional policies have attempted to minimize conflict.

IV. *Changing Patterns of Race Relations in the International System*

Because of the breakdown of subjection and assimilation as regulative factors in international race relations, the tendency is toward intensification of racial conflict and *increasing* transnational racial ties. Since Europeans united in a common bond of whiteness to dominate the black, brown, and yellow peoples of the world, men have been attempting to join in the bond of color across national lines to pursue racially justified (if not always racist) causes. The Pan-African Movement, formed after black African resistance had failed to curb white intrusion into Africa, is probably the best-documented transnational racial grouping organized to counter white dominance. Black men of different nationalities and cultures, and speaking different languages, joined in pan-Negro organizations to win humane treatment, then equality, and finally independence for their black brothers in Africa. Out of this movement grew the race-conscious philosophies of Negritude and the African Personality—philosophies of color which black men had never before felt a need to formulate.

Although political independence has been won by most black African states, the influences of white dominance still linger in varying degrees. Economic dependence, in particular, is a major point of continuing con-

[8] Halpern, *op.cit.*, p. 14.

flict as indicated by the tensions over nationalization of Euro-American foreign investments.

The 1955 Bandung Conference of African and Asian peoples was the first international meeting explicitly called to unite "peoples of color" against white domination and oppression. Specifically referring to racial differences, China successfully kept the U.S.S.R. out of the Bandung meeting, making it an international conference of non-white peoples. The policies of racial discrimination in South Africa and the U.K. increasingly are causing Indians and other Asians in those countries to refer to themselves as black—black symbolizing a transcendence of nationality, religion, culture, and sex—in order to combat white dominance. History also provides much evidence of transnational white collaboration in support of white domination over non-white peoples.

Trends. The centripetal racial system was not conducive to transnational linkages between subordinate racial groups. Its domestic assimilationist thrusts minimized attempts at transnational racial ties which were largely rejected by non-whites, e.g., Marcus Garvey and his "back to Africa" movement in the U.S. As a consequence, the foreign policies of states with these types of systems unabashedly reflected the racist assumptions and interests of their white dominant groups; for example, President Woodrow Wilson and Jan Christian Smuts, Prime Minister of South Africa, joined together at Versailles to defeat the Japanese plea for a covenant on racial equality.

In contrast, the centrifugal stage of domestic race relations tends to encourage outside intervention as subordinate groups seek aid for their rebellion or secession. The incipient pattern of racial pluralism that characterizes the centrifugal stage encourages non-white transnational movements to strengthen the identity ties and cultural accomplishments of their group. Illustrative of this is the Mexican-American of the Southwest whose militant groups increasingly identify with the nationalist movements of Puerto Rico and Latin America. The foreign policy response of white dominance states to this phase is more accommodating, since they both fear and respect the new forces that have become domestically important.

A central proposition is that *centripetal (assimilationist) racial patterns have had a strong influence on the development of expansionist and imperialistic foreign policies while centrifugal pressures promote revolution against white dominance.* Obviously, additional factors such as economic exploitation may produce imperialism. But the relationship of racial stratification to the development of social Darwinism in the 19th century is substantiating evidence of the development of racism as a rationale for imperialism. The "primitiveness of non-white races" and the "superiority of Euro-American religious and political forms" are notions related to the motive and rationale for colonization which found their zenith in the Victorian era.[9] The "civilizing mission" of the British, French, and Germans was, in the eyes of the European upper classes, a justification for the subjection of Africa in the 19th century. And the U.S. sense of Manifest Destiny in the Pacific was an important influence in the acquisition of the Philippines.[10] The origins of these racist ideas can be traced to the dominant white Western elites. Black men did serve in empires, as in the case of the French Governor of Senegal, Blaise Diagne, prior to World War I. However, these were assimilated Africans, or what South Africans would call "honorary whites," because they accepted the values and practices of dominant whites. The fact was that the ruling elites were white and Western and arrogantly confident of their mission to bring order, commerce, Christianity, and their particular culture to the "inferior peoples."

The historic expansion of the U.S.S.R. in Asia is a pattern of white assimilationist imperialism. Today this plays a part in the Sino-Soviet conflict along with ideological and geographical factors. There is much evidence that the U.S.S.R. today exhibits what we would describe as a disintegrative conflict pattern toward its own minorities, despite claims to non-racialism and multi-nationalism. The treatment of its Jewish minority is the outstanding example of this centrifugal pattern of incoherence.[11] Marxist states, despite their theoretical elimination of the class struggle, do not always abolish the racial struggle with their class revolution, but do create severe internal and external tensions by their mythology of multi-nationalism which intensifies the drive of subordinate groups for genuine self-determination. The Sino-Soviet conflict within the international communist movement is in large part the result of white dominance of the non-white world now in revolt over values and power distribution.

South Africa is in a stage of transition from a centripetal racist system to a centrifugal one. The power of subjection is so great that racial identification is still regulative rather than disintegrative. Until they were

[9] Ali Mazrui, "Post Imperial Fragmentation: The Legacy of Ethnic and Racial Conflict," *Studies in Race and Nations,* Vol. 1, No. 2 (1969) Center on International Race Relations, GSIS, University of Denver.

[10] William A. Williams quoted William Jennings Bryan as saying, "The Filipinos cannot be citizens without endangering our civilization," in *The Tragedy of American Diplomacy* (Cleveland, Ohio: World Publishing Co., 1959), p. 36. Americans therefore had to civilize them.

[11] Edy Kaufman, "The Jews in Russia," *Race Today* (March, 1970), pp. 67-75.

banned, the nationalist movements were highly European-oriented and non-racial in values. They sought a common citizenship for all races based on Euro-American principles of government. This attitude still predominates among most non-whites, but given the influence of Black Power spokesmen and secessionist movements, this attitude is changing.[12]

In South Africa the separate development policy of the government has projected deceptive multi-national goals, such as the establishment of separate nationhood through Bantustans, and the granting of nominal independence to Lesotho, Botswana, and Swaziland. This independence is a myth. The reality for the vast majority of non-whites, whose numbers are growing very rapidly, is continued subjection to the industrialized economy and marginal assimilation into the consumption patterns of urban life, while the standard-of-living gap grows.

Despite subjection of the masses, there has begun, among a minority of black South Africans, secessionist movements which are strong precipitating forces for revolution and racial war. Thus, Bantustan leaders, such as Chief Buthelezi, hope to achieve independence, and exiled revolutionaries gather in increasing numbers on the boundaries to attack South Africa from without and organize resistance within.

South Africa's foreign policy reflects this transitional movement from a centripetal to a centrifugal pattern of race relations. Ruled since the 1950's by the blatantly racist Afrikaners, an imperialistic South Africa has acquired territory (Namibia) and used financial power to penetrate markets in the independent African states. The country's military boundaries have been extended recently into the Portuguese territories and into Rhodesia.[13] An active program of seeking client African states ready to accept South African loans and trade by a policy of "dialogue" and "contacts" has begun. In addition, South Africa has sought closer military ties with Euro-American powers through arms purchases.

While her imperialistic expansion is characteristic of centripetal systems, the rapid expansion of South Africa's military forces is indicative of the fears characteristic of the centrifugal pattern. Euro-American powers have needed far greater military power in this defensive process than during imperialistic expansion. South Africa's attempts to join the NATO alliance further indicate her desire for white assistance. At the same time a low level of racial war has begun along her extended boundaries where

[12] Newell M. Stultz, "The Politics of Security: South Africa under Verwoerd, 1961-66," *The Journal of Modern African Studies,* Vol. 7, No. 1, pp. 3-21. See also Gwendolen Carter, "Multi-racialism in Africa," *International Affairs,* Vol. 34, No. 4, pp. 437-463.

[13] Richard Stevens, "South Africa and Independent Black Africa" *Africa Today,* Vol. 17, No. 3 (May-June, 1970), pp. 25-32.

African states support liberation movements. South Africa also seeks to assist Portugal and Rhodesia in defeating the black liberation movements. Continuous treason trials at home and desperate attempts to organize multi-national Bantustans are all indicators of the conflict and incoherence that now characterize the domestic politics underlying South Africa's foreign relations.

Under the centrifugal pressures of non-white resistance, the assimilationist system becomes incoherent and this in turn develops a new set of foreign policy pressures. Threatened by a significant secessionist movement which promises civil war, a state becomes especially sensitive to the dangers of foreign intervention. This shifts the emphasis from expansionism to an inwardly-directed militarization. Efforts are made to placate those who might intervene on behalf of the racial secessionists, and external military assistance is sought to suppress rebellion. This pattern persists where white domination of non-white people continues and becomes more rigid because of non-white centrifugal pressures and white failures to reform or compromise.

The best example of a white dominant system which has reached the secessionist stage can be found in Portuguese Africa, where the claim over the "Portuguese Provinces of Africa" is widely disputed by the rebellions of liberation forces in Guinea-Bissau, Angola, and Mozambique. Through NATO, Portugal has obtained outside assistance to repress the secessionists and actively seeks diplomatic support from Latin American and Asian states. Its racially-based *assimilado* policy for Africans is producing the same reaction which the French assimilation policy produced in Indochina and Africa:[14] increased rebellion and growing outside intervention.

Secessionist conflicts arising from the centrifugal stage of incoherence are very dangerous in the modern world, particularly if great powers sometimes utilize them either to maintain their presence in an area or to dislodge an antagonist. As the South African and Rhodesian racial patterns move directly into the disintegration phase of irreconcilable conflict, they become prime targets for interventionary cold war tactics. Here lies one of the gravest dangers to world peace.

The U.S. has also moved into the centrifugal conflict phase. Racist war abroad and minority rebellion at home have created a major racial crisis in which domestic and foreign policy cannot be distinguished clearly. During the centripetal period of domestic assimilation and Darwinian colo-

---

[14] See "Allies in Empire," *Africa Today,* Vol. 17, No. 4 (July-August, 1970).

nial expansion abroad, the U.S. attempted to build a *Pax Pacifica.* Pre-World War II rivalries with Japan, the post-war intervention of the U.S. in the Chinese civil war, and the two wars the U.S. has fought in Korea and Vietnam have been influenced by domestic racial assimilationist attitudes and external paternalistic power patterns originally structured in the 19th century. The post-World War II assumption that peace depended upon American political and military presence on the Asian mainland and the islands of the Pacific has a racial dimension closely akin to the imperialistic rule of the British Raj. Early involvement in the Indochina War arose out of the power vacuum caused by French decolonialization. The U.S. leadership believed this would be filled by the Communists. However, the attempt to launch a crusade against Communism for Asian self-determination reflected the same kind of racist assumption that underlay the concept of the "white man's burden" in the League's Mandate system—a system first suggested by President Wilson.

The racial aspects of the Vietnam conflict clearly emerged as a form of genocide as the war expanded. American militarists refused to believe that "coolies" could stand up to saturation bombing and pressed for a victory despite humanitarian protests. Indisputable proof of the racial paranoia of American society which sustained these policies was the widespread outcry of support for Lt. Calley when even the Army sought to condemn him to life imprisonment for his "wasting" of Vietnamese civilian lives.

The centrifugal phase in American society and foreign policy has only begun as a result of the rise of minority militancy which has been greatly accelerated by the Vietnam disaster. Black and Chicano movements have been joined by young Asians in protesting the "white man's war" and the particular "racist" exploitation of minorities to fight it. The growing disaffection of these minorities has already had a considerable impact upon the expansionist policies of the U.S. American white dominance leadership is sensitive to the penetration possibilities of foreign adversaries, as J. Edgar Hoover's remarks concerning the security threat of immigrant Chinese demonstrated. And the white urban middle class is increasingly anxious to quell the restlessness of the ghettos. Therefore, the political power of those advocating disengagement and reduction of American power abroad has been enhanced by the disenchantment of non-white minorities with the melting pot myth and with their tendency to identify with non-whites abroad in clashes against American power. It is too early to predict whether this will set in motion forces capable of finally curbing the considerable American corporate interests in Latin America and

Southern Africa, but the revolutionary black workers of Polaroid have surfaced a conflict of interests with explosive potential in American politics and foreign policy.

Resolution of major domestic racial issues would mean the movement from centrifugal disintegration and conflict into a pluralistic consensus in which race was no longer a significant stratification indicator. This can begin either as a result of an equalitarian revolution, which removes white dominance, or secession, which establishes a uni-racial state. There are no pure societies of this type in the world today, but they may well emerge out of the centrifugal conflict era.

In pluralistic societies centripetal imperialism would be non-existent, and the tendency toward the militarism and paranoia of the centrifugal race pattern would also disappear. By removing discrimination at home, such societies would also contain a high level of respect and recognition for non-white cultures and peoples. This would tend to strengthen the humanistic factors in foreign policy as against the corporate and security factors which have predominated to date. Much less certain would be the consequences of secession since such new states might carry with them the seeds of racial imperialism from which they had escaped.

Sweden, where only the Lapps are affected adversely by racial status, is moving in the direction of racial pluralism. A great asset for Swedish foreign policy is its long history of neutrality and imperial abstention. The Swedes have directly assisted liberation movements in Africa, an important new departure for a white dominance system. Perhaps this is indicative of a relationship between non-racialism at home and anti-apartheid abroad.

Subsystems and Race. Since the early 1950's, at the regional subsystem level,[15] centrifugal forces in racial patterns have injected conflict which contributes to colonial wars and secessions. European nations have granted independence to African states rather than fight protracted colonial wars. More recently the identification patterns of subordinate minorities have emerged, cutting across national lines, particularly among the blacks within the Atlantic subsystem which is a prime example of a racially stratified white dominant system.[16] The white NATO powers (excluding Greece and Turkey) form its core group and dominate the system, while non-NATO white powers such as those in white dominated Southern Afri-

[15] Michael Banks, "Sub-systems and Regional Studies," *International Studies Quarterly* (Winter, 1970).
[16] L. Centori and S. Spiegel in *The International Politics of Regions: A Comparative Approach* (New York: Prentice-Hall, 1970). Their model included Europe but did not develop it

ca comprise the peripheral area of the subsystem. The Atlantic subsystem demonstrates a high degree of integration in terms of standard interaction variables as well as race.[17] In fact, racial stratification patterns account in large measure for the coordination of political and economic policies within the subsystem and explain in part the magnitude of mutual support between white states in the North and South Atlantic to the exclusion of the non-white.

In the modern centrifugal era, the racial factor alienates and even precipitates rebellion against the prevailing policies of the dominant powers in the Atlantic subsystem. The growing alignment of subordinate black groups within the system with sympathetic outside states, both African and communist, is indicative of potential conflicts in the future. The link-up with rebellious groups is not limited to states outside of the subsystem. There is a growing identification between Black Power and colored dissidence within the core group of states, including the revolutionary forces of Southern Africa on the periphery.

The effect of the growth of this black identity bloc in close proximity to the U.S. and cutting across U.S. relations with Latin America, may have significant implications for future relations. The growth of Black Power movements in the Caribbean is a trend that may greatly affect the future.

The Global System. Race thus operates as a stratification device for the entire world system in which the powerful white dominant nations have long predominated. Eastern Europe is joined with the white Atlantic regional subsystem to create a world racial pattern of white dominance. The attitude of the white states of the world is in part a reflection of their own internal stratification problems. There appears to be a direct relationship between the severity of these internal racial problems and the defensiveness or openness of a white nation's policy toward the non-white world, as reflected by support for human rights conventions and international collective action to abolish discriminatory practices within and between nations.[18]

International racial stratification can be seen in terms of international mobility and opportunity. Here, poverty statistics, development trends, population growth, and international migration all point to a very rigid

as an Atlantic system including the U.S.

[17] Unpublished paper by G. W. Shepherd, Jr., "The White Atlantic Subsystem and Black Southern Africa," delivered to a UCLA symposium in April, 1970.

[18] While the ratification of human rights conventions by the small non-white powers leaves much to be desired, it is a substantially superior record to the U.S. and South Africa. See "Acceptance of Human Rights Treaties," UNITAR, A/Conf 32/15, 28 March 1968, Annex 11.

global system of distribution. Race is the most important factor determining the life chances of any child born into this world. This, coupled with the militaristic and conflict-prone policies of white dominance states, projects conflict, not stability.

The formation of the U.N. and other world organizations has enabled the non-white peoples to gain greater participation within the international system. Yet even an Afro-Asian majority within the U.N. does not change the realities of international stratification in the distribution of rewards. The basic decisions regarding the world economy are still made by the white dominance nations, as the GATT conferences have clearly shown. Communist China's hostility to the current Euro-American domination of the U.N. and the world system is not simply ideological, but is also a protest, with power, on behalf of the colonized majority whose color has been for centuries a sign of weakness. The racial stratification pattern which maintains power and control in the hands of the white dominance nations of the world is bound to be a source of hostility and conflict.

And modification of this racial basis of international conflict in the future probably will be achieved best by the development of racial pluralism in white dominance powers. These states might then be able to lead an attack upon international racial inequities provided time has not run out.

The lack of determination by the most powerful nations of the world to reform the international system significantly through economic development programs or changes in trade patterns has frequently been attacked. There is a remarkable decline in international aid while GNP rises in the U.S. and other white dominance systems—an indication of their inability to sympathize with the "have-not" nations. It may be that fear is a more compelling stimulus to reform than empathy, and that real redistribution and reform will come about only with the growth of revolutionary racial conflict.

The racially pluralist pattern is clearly the ideal for the international system, as well as individual state systems. Guidelines for redirection can be taken from this pattern, which must create mobility and greater life chances for all, as well as redistribute power. Any prospect for preventing growing racial conflict is linked to radical changes within the white dominance systems themselves. The questions of time and pace are acute. Dominant groups, however, tend to lack either the vision or the determination to turn the disastrous possibilities into more hopeful prospects.